Discovering Truth
in a Changing World

Discovering Truth in a Changing World

Lesslie Newbigin

Alpha International
London

Published by Alpha International
Holy Trinity Brompton
Brompton Road, London, SW7 1JA

Contents

Foreword

I first met Bishop Lesslie Newbigin when he came one evening to a concert at Holy Trinity Brompton, which was being given by the New English Orchestra. I asked somewhat diffidently if he would ever be willing to find time to come and talk to us as a church. He instantly and very graciously agreed.

In this way started an association over several years which was of enormous benefit to us and which led to a warmth and friendship with myself and the church that he was kind enough to express both publicly and privately until his death.

He was involved in world Christianity for well over half a century and, after spending nearly 40 years as a missionary in India, instead of retiring to a quiet life in the country, he went to serve in an inner city Birmingham parish.

There was certainly a prophetic anointing on him – for instance, his wisdom and insight in sensing that the beginning of the twenty-first century would see a clash between Western materialism and fundamentalist Islam. And I find it extraordinary to think that in *The Household of God* he so clearly identified the major streams of world Christianity – the Catholic, Protestant and Charismatic – so far ahead of time.

He was such a warm and wise figure. He had such a passion for and commitment to the church. In contrast to the timidity or anxiety of many Christians in the West, Bishop Lesslie's renewed confidence was in the gospel of Jesus Christ and a passionate desire to bring it into the public square. It is of course the story he had come to see as true above all other stories. It is the only story through which humanity and history can be understood. It is the only story that, in its ending foreshadowed in Christ's resurrection, holds out hope for the world. It is the story that had shaped him and in which he lived. It is the story that he brought to life with consummate skill and applied to every aspect of not only church life, but also the wider culture of the world. It is this story that he articulated at our School of Theology between 1994–5, and which forms the basis of this book. 'Here it is,' he seemed to be saying, 'guard it, live it, proclaim it.'

Our hope is that this book will inspire many to do just that.

Sandy Millar
Vicar, Holy Trinity Brompton

CHAPTER ONE

How Do We Know?

Because this discussion is about Christian doctrine we
should perhaps start by looking closely at the whole
business of how do we 'know'?

Many people think the Christian faith is not something
you 'know' but only something that you 'believe'. In our
culture, knowing and believing are supposed to be different
from each other. So, this is the point where we should make
a start.

In our present culture there is a strange belief that doubt
is somehow more honest than faith. This belief suggests that
faith might lead you astray, and that doubt is the mark of an
honest inquirer. This, of course, is nonsense. Both faith and
doubt have proper parts to play in the business of knowing.
But faith is primary.

You cannot know anything unless you begin by believing.
This beginning means opening your eyes, trusting the evidence of your senses and being aware of a world beyond
yourself. We can only begin to 'know' something when there
is this initial act of faith.

We might later come to doubt some of the things we first
believed. We cannot believe everything, but doubt is only

1

possible on the basis of something that we believe. I could make a statement and you might doubt its truth. I could then ask you why you doubted it, and you would reply, 'Because I believe something else.' I could follow this by saying, 'But I doubt that.' There is no rational doubt except on the basis of faith. So faith is primary and doubt secondary.

One of the consequences of this contemporary fashion, of regarding doubt as more honest than faith, is that it leads to a profound conservatism. This is because in every society there is what sociologists call a 'plausibility structure'. There exists a whole pattern of beliefs that in general nobody questions. It is taken for granted that this is how everything is and everybody knows and accepts the situation. If something is proposed which seems to contradict that plausibility structure, then we doubt it. So when doubt is put primarily above faith it means that we tend to accept what everybody else believes. It is a profoundly conservative approach and is not – as is often thought – a radical shift.

I have often imagined meeting a native of one of the high mountain valleys of Papua New Guinea where they have never met anyone of European descent and have never heard anything of our ideas. I could imagine telling them of a tribe of white-skinned blue-eyed people living on an offshore island on the other side of the world.

If I told them that these offshore islanders believe that the universe came into existence by a series of accidents and that although it works in a beautiful and orderly way, it was designed by nobody and for no purpose, they would probably say, 'They must be a very superstitious tribe!' It simply would not fit their plausibility structure. But those assumptions, which I have perhaps caricatured a little, are those that govern the thinking of many of our contemporaries. So faith is primary and doubt secondary. Both are necessary.

In our Western culture we have developed and relied upon the use of 'science' which, of course, means knowledge. Science is only another word for 'knowing' but we have separated science from other kinds of knowing in the belief that science gives us what is called 'objective facts' and that things which cannot qualify in that sense are of necessity purely subjective.

This again is a fashion of thought, and an absurd one, because there can be no knowing of anything without a knowing subject. If there is no subjectivity there is no knowledge. So the idea of purely objective knowledge is an illusion, but a most powerful one.

I was once trying to communicate my faith to a young man who finally told me, 'Well, of course, that's just what you think.' The reply to that must surely be, 'Well, did anyone ever find out anything without thinking?' The idea that there is somehow a kind of knowledge which is not what you think, but something quite independent of your thinking, is absurd – but it is a prime and dominant illusion of Western culture.

There has to be a knowing subject and that subject is, by definition, someone moulded by a particular culture and shaped by his or her own psychological make-up.

Furthermore, knowing is not something that just happens

to us. It is something we have to achieve, a skill we have to try to learn and in which we may succeed or fail.

Knowing in this respect is a learned achievement that requires our commitment. It is not like a photographic image but rather it is a skill and indeed an achievement that we have to accomplish.

In addition, we only learn by apprenticeship to a tradition of knowing. First there are the established practices and conventions embodied in language. We learn as small children to speak a language which is an apprenticeship into a tradition, a way of perceiving or grasping reality and no knowing is possible without that. This is supremely true of science. Science is profoundly conservative and traditional. No one is accepted as a scientist competent to undertake independent research without undergoing years of apprenticeship in the traditions of scientific method.

How can we be certain that the things we 'know' are really true? This is the momentous point at which, I think, the famous French philosopher René Descartes (1596–1650) led us astray. Descartes lived in a time of scepticism. He inaugurated the seventeenth century intellectual revolution that laid down the foundation for what we think of as the 'modern' scientific age.

Descartes was convinced that by following the method that he adopted – the method that has guided science ever since – it would be possible to have more than what he would have called mere belief, but instead to have certainties, certain knowledge. He approached this in three stages. He started first with something he could not doubt, his own existence. Descartes wrote, 'Even if I am doubting, that means that I am thinking, and if I am thinking, I exist. [*Cogito, ergo sum*] I think, therefore, I am. That is certain.'

By various arguments, with the precision and certainty of mathematics, he set out to build upon that certainty a body of certain or indubitable truth. That was the second step. Finally he developed what is known as 'The Critical Principle'. This has been the jewel in the crown of Western culture ever since. It is the principle that all claims to knowledge must be tested by those two criteria and anything which falls short of certainty in that sense is not knowledge, but only belief. And as the great philosopher John Locke asserted, belief 'is a persuasion which falls short of knowledge.'

So when we stand up in church and affirm, 'I believe' what we are really saying, by Locke's definition, is that we do not know. Belief is therefore considered something other than knowledge. Knowledge is something that is absolutely certain on the basis of the method that Descartes laid down. It is this ground upon which our so-called modern scientific world has been built.

But for the same reason that I suggested when I talked about doubt, Descartes' critical method was bound for eventual destruction. The Critical Principle has to be subject to the Critical Principle itself. It is obvious that you can only criticise a statement on the ground of comparing it with something else which you believe. So it is always possible to turn this critical scrutiny round on that basis and criticise it.

5

So it is hardly surprising that in the centuries of philosophy following Descartes there has been a descent into increasing scepticism.

David Hume (1711–76), the Scottish philosopher, demolished most of the principles of Descartes. Immanuel Kant (1724–1804), who was the professor of logic and metaphysics at the University of Königsberg, East Prussia, tried to restore the grounds for certain knowledge, but had to conclude that we cannot know ultimate reality and that it must be beyond our knowledge. But how Kant knew that, one does not know! Finally, the German philosopher Friedrich Nietzsche (1844–1900) saw with terrible clarity that to continue in the direction that European culture had taken would lead inevitably and inexorably to the point where we could no longer speak of truth or falsehood, nor of good or bad. Any claim to know the truth would be an exercise of dominance. The only thing that would be certain is the will, and any claim to truth would have to be regarded as a claim to dominance, to power.

As a result, we have relapsed into what is now called 'postmodernism', a sinking into the kind of belief where people say, 'Well, it may be true for you, but it's not true for me.' It is believed that there is no such thing as objective truth. In the field of science there is still a good deal of confidence in the idea of objective truth, but even in this area it has been increasingly eroded.

We have actually reached the point where – with the so-called deconstruction movement in literary criticism – the idea that any text has any meaning of itself is demolished. The ultimate development of that is in the work of Don Cupitt, who simply states: 'Words are purely culture constructions and do not themselves correspond to any reality.' So when we say, 'I believe in God' we are expressing a kind of subjective feeling, but there is no reality to which those words correspond.

It is true that all truth claims are the result of cultural influence. The English language is just one of many languages of the world and if I make a truth claim, I am using this particular language to express or suggest statements of truth that relate or belong to the culture implicit in that language. Where are we if we probe the relationship between words and those things which are not words? Do the words 'I believe in God' correspond to a reality which is not words? Is it not obvious that the relation between words and those things which are not words cannot be a matter of words? It must be something different. And this is where the profound error of Descartes' thinking becomes clear. Descartes, who has been followed by three centuries of Western thought, conceived the human mind as though it was a disembodied objective eye looking at the world in a disinterested or impartial way. It was as if the mind was not part of the world at all and was looking at it from outside and therefore able to take an objective view – not a view shaped by any particular personal thoughts, feelings or cultural influences.

That detached, or objective view, is of course absurd. The mind is not a disembodied entity; it is part of us. Any knowing that we have of anything arises out of our bodily engagement in the actual business of the world. There is no other way by which we can come to know anything and we test our beliefs about what is the case by acting upon them.

One can see in the simplest of ways how a child learns to understand the world. If a balloon is brought closer to a baby, then that balloon has apparently become bigger. It takes a long time before a baby can understand the idea of distance and perception and it does this by taking hold of objects and feeling them with its hands. In this way you can see a baby exploring the world. If its eyes do not tell it all the truth then it uses its hands. It is only by being embodied in the actuality of the world that we begin to understand it.

We are part of this world which we seek to know. The vast delusion that we have suffered since the work of Descartes is the idea that we are somehow at one remove from it with a kind of spectator's privilege of looking at the world from outside. This non-committed view does not allow the influence of personal commitments or personal interests. Objective knowledge is supposed to be that kind of knowledge.

That is a God's-eye view of the world and we do not have that privileged position. We are a part of the world and everything in it, and our knowing relates to our actual bodily engagement as we try to understand and cope with its reality.

Let us look a little more deeply into what I have called the 'structure of knowing'. Take a piece of paper with writing on it. The lines are just ink marks on a white sheet. That is all they are, from one point of view. When we learn to read we have at first to pay an awful lot of attention to the actual shapes of these ink marks. We have long since passed the time when we even look at the shape of those letters. We have moved on to attend to the meaning they communicate.

This 'from to' structure is fundamental to all our knowing. If we look at a picture with a magnifying glass we see tiny daubs of paint here and there, but it is only when we stand back that we see it as a coherent whole. We see the picture, not by ignoring the little paint marks, but precisely by an action of our mind that integrates all these little markings into a united whole – the single picture. Similarly, the marks of ink on the page are integrated by our minds into a meaning, and we attend to the meaning from these subsidiary clues, of which we are normally quite unconscious. While we are learning to read we have to attend to the clues and, of course, it is an effort, a struggle, to learn. But once we have learnt these clues there is a tacit unconscious integration of them into a whole structure of meaning that crosses an enormous range of our knowing.

The learning of language is one of the first examples of the way we learn by 'apprenticeship' to a tradition. As we go on, we learn words, concepts, models, pictures, theories and hypotheses which to begin with are often strange to us. Asking the question: 'What does this concept mean?' we have to attend to it in the same way the small child pays attention to forming letters while learning to read.

When we have mastered these things, then they become the subsidiaries from which we attend to the focal meaning.

And, in that sense, we 'indwell' the tradition. All of our knowing involves indwelling our bodily senses. I am able to see a group of people only because my retina is stimulated by light in various ways. I am not conscious of the process but it is from this process that I attend to the meaning of what I am looking at.

So we have a threefold structure of knowing. First there are the subsidiaries from which you attend to the focal meaning, and all our learning then involves us in new efforts to integrate a great number of subsidiaries into that focal meaning. So there are the subsidiaries and then the focal meaning. The third element is what I call the 'heuristic passion'. As I said, knowing does not happen automatically. We have to struggle and that struggle involves trying to find meaning and coherence in all these different and apparently separate details.

This third element, heuristic passion, is the desire and longing to know. It is something we share with animals. One can observe an animal puzzled by something it has never previously seen and watch it as it struggles to discover what it is. This passionate desire to know and to find out things for oneself is fundamental to our nature and something we undoubtedly share with the animal world.

This means that we have to take seriously the personal factors involved in all knowing. Science proceeds by a whole series of personal efforts which involve intuition, a kind of sense that there is a pattern in these apparently meaningless and random facts. There is an intuition that there is something there which can be seen as a meaningful whole.

There is the imagination which can frame a possible picture, a hypothesis of how things are. There exists the patience that can go on, year after year, trying to solve a difficult problem, sometimes failing right up to the end. Einstein spent the last years of his life trying to establish a credible and workable theory that would unify relativity and quantum physics, and failed.

The heuristic passion and courage of Einstein governed the closing years of his life. And what of courage? This involves the willingness to take risks, as Einstein did, because there is always the risk of failure. All of these profoundly personal factors are involved in the business of knowing, and the strange idea that knowing is something that does not involve these subjective elements, that it is something purely objective, is nonsense.

But if you say that, then how do we know that we are in actual contact with the truth? I have emphasised the subjectivity of our knowing but what about its objectivity? How can we or do we know that as a result of all this we are actually connecting with reality?

In this respect I think there are at least three topics that deserve our consideration. The first token of reality is a sense of meaning. When a scientist struggles to make sense of a whole lot of apparently random data, and suddenly sees a picture that holds it all together, then the conviction occurs that something true has been discovered. The sense of

11

meaning and beauty, of symmetry and coherence – these are the first tests of objectivity.

The second test, of course, is that the scientist publishes these findings and invites other scientists to consider their worth – their truth. This is relevant to the whole question of Christian mission and evangelism. Any belief that we are not prepared to publish is not a real belief. If we believe something to be true, then we must publish it because its truth is universal.

Thirdly, if something is true, it will lead to further truths. This is crucial. Any real discovery will always lead the researcher, the searcher or the scientist onwards towards further discoveries. Many dedicated people have spent years in search of the solution to some problem which led them nowhere. Think of those long centuries spent by thinkers trying to understand the nature of gravity in relation to perpetual motion, or to produce the philosopher's stone which would turn dross into gold. These attempts over hundreds of years have ended in nothing but failure.

The mark of truth is that it always leads on to further truth. And so that gives us a dynamic picture of knowledge, in contrast to the one that Descartes gave us. He, like most of the philosophers of science following him, conceived truth as something buttoned up and complete. There were no doubts or no uncertainties. It was a kind of static picture of truth, something which could only be possible 'from above'.

But a working scientist will give you a different picture of truth. That person knows that there is yet more to be discovered. The test of the truthfulness of what has been discovered is not that there is nothing else to be learned but precisely that it leads onward into further reaches of reality. This is what I would call an epistemology 'from below'. The word epistemology simply means 'the science of knowing' – how do we know anything? It comes from the Greek word *episteme* – knowing.

There is a kind of epistemology 'from above' where, as a philosopher, one looks down on truth claims and judges whether or not they can be sustained. But there is also an epistemology 'from below' which is the way that the scientists actually work, where they know that they have not arrived at the final truth and are always pressing forward and seeking more. But the test that they have made contact with reality will be that they are led on to further discoveries. It is a dynamic conception of truth, unlike that of Descartes.

And so we arrive at an important new area of consideration. I have previously been writing about knowing in the sense that scientists talk about it: knowing the natural world, the world of things. But there is another kind of knowing, which is the knowing of persons. In many languages there are two different verbs to express this notion. In German the verb *wissen* means to know things and *kennen* means to know people. In French *savoir* means knowing things while *connaître* means knowing people. Unfortunately in English there is only one such word, but there is an acknowledged difference between the kind of knowing where the object is a thing and the knowing of a person.

13

If it is a thing that cannot answer back then I decide what to do about it. I can put it on the laboratory table and dissect it. I can put it through various tests and decide the questions to be asked. I am in control. That is one kind of knowing. But we also know that there is another kind of knowing, coming to know a person. In one sense, you can dissect a person on the operating table and discover how the body works, but then you lose the chance of getting to know that person!

This other kind of knowing is where the object is a subject. The object of my knowing is himself or herself, a subject. Therefore, I am not in full control. If I am to know that person I must be prepared to be questioned myself. I must put my trust in that person. I must be willing to open up and trust that this person is speaking the truth. There is no other way to get to know a person. So here we use faith in a second sense. They are not two separate senses.

At the beginning of this chapter I wrote that we do not know anything except by an initial act of faith. That is faith considered in its cognitive aspect, that is to say as a way of knowing. But faith also has an affective or emotional aspect; it is more a way of loving, of relationship with another.

Now these two are not separate, but they are two different dimensions of faith. So the question is: 'How are these two moulds of knowing related to each other?' Obviously they are not separate. We do not get to know a person as a disembodied spirit but rather through the acts of speaking and gesture, the actuality of events in this physical world by which people makes themselves known to one another. That point is fundamental.

A machine's correct mechanical functioning and structure depends on the skill of the person who built it just as much as it depends upon the quality of the metals and components that went into its construction. It depends on the physics and chemistry of its parts and the competent mechanical design of the person who made it possible.

But if you come across a machine you have never seen before, you can examine it to your heart's content but you will never discover its purpose unless you are told by the maker or by someone who has learned from the maker, how to use it. In other words, the mechanical structure of the machine provides the conditions under which the machine works, but does not provide its meaning or purpose. This belongs to a different level of logic.

If I may return to the context of knowing persons, neurosurgery, for example, has developed enormously in the past few years and doctors can now examine the brain and understand better, with amazing surgical precision, how its complex electrical circuits and synaptic connections work. But no matter how far the neurosurgeon might go in this anatomical and physiological analysis of brain function, it would not tell that surgeon a single thing about what the subject thought or felt. There is no possible way it could. It is a different logical level. Consequently, there is a hierarchy of logical levels in all our knowing.

The laws of chemistry depend upon the laws of physics

but physics can never replace chemistry. The laws of mechanics depend upon the laws of physics and chemistry but mechanics cannot be replaced by physics and chemistry. Biology in this sense depends upon all three theoretical laws because a bird or an animal is also, in one sense, a mechanism. Creatures function because they are chemically composed of hard and soft tissue – muscles and blood and so forth – and these tissues in turn comprise the atomic structure of the animal. But neither physics, chemistry nor mechanics can replace biology. There exists a hierarchy of levels, and each level can never fully explain the true function of the higher one.

It is therefore clear that in viewing humanity there is a level above the physical, chemical, mechanical and biological level. You cannot really explain a human being. You cannot come to know a person in the sense that we normally use this term of 'knowing', simply by knowing the physical, chemical, biological and mechanical working of the body. The attempt to explain things on a logical level lower than the appropriate one is known as reductionism and it could be said that the whole of the past three centuries of the so-called modern or scientific view of the world has been an example of reductionism – of trying to explain reality on logical levels, on lower levels than those that are appropriate.

The relevance of all this will emerge later, but in the meantime let us consider that most famous of conundrums in this whole business of knowing as propounded by Plato, who asked these questions: 'What does it mean to seek truth?

Is truth something that we know or something that we do not know? If we know truth, why do we seek it? If we do not know it, how can we recognise it when we find it?'

Plato's answer was to invoke the prevailing doctrine of reincarnation. His answer was that essentially truth was recognised, known and remembered from a person's previous incarnation. Today few people accept Plato's explanation, and yet scientists go on their merry way making 'discoveries' without attempting to answer the conundrum: 'What does it mean to search for truth? What does it mean when people talk of the love of truth?'

As I said earlier, heuristic passion is the third component in all our knowing – the passion to understand and find meaning in apparent meaninglessness. So is it not at least possible that heuristic passion is a response in us to something beyond us which draws out that passion?

Research scientist Michael Polanyi (1891–1976) was an academic with many discoveries to his credit. He struggled with Plato's conundrum and felt himself to be drawn onward. He was propelled forward by an intuitive feeling that there was something further to be found, as if there was some hidden meaning, beauty or coherence, in the things that baffled him both as a research scientist and as a human being. He felt himself as a scientist being drawn forward beyond the point of being a scientist. Heuristic passion is a response to something prior to us, touching one of the central truths of our being.

This brings us in a sense to the limits of philosophy. The

17

Christian faith affirms that the ultimate logical level upon which things are to be understood is neither physical, chemical, biological, nor mechanical, but the personal, and that our whole existence can only be understood if we take this personal level into account. If that is true, then everything will depend upon whether the one who is the person whose purpose governs all things has revealed that purpose to us. And that, of course, is what the gospel affirms.

Whereas Muslims, for example maintain that God has simply dictated the truth for us to take it or leave it, the gospel affirms that God's revelation of himself is an action in which truth and grace go together, where truth and love are one. God's self-revelation of himself is exactly what this argument would suggest – something which draws us to himself. And if that is true, then we have to conclude that this is the secret both of knowing and being.

Our knowing is not separate from our being. If this is true (and that is what the gospel affirms to be true) then there is something that causes the acorn to grow into an oak and not a cabbage, or a foetus to become a human being and not a monster. That something which has drawn forth the whole process of evolution is not, as Darwin thought, the result of chance mutations operating from below, but is the response of the created order to the one who has created it and who calls all creation to its proper fulfilment.

This would mean that the heuristic passion at the heart of our knowing is a response to God's calling upon us. Alone in creation we are conscious of this calling to seek the truth and to seek it in him. So contrary to Descartes, we are not dealing with disembodied ideas.

The truth can only be known through incarnation, through the actual presence of God in history, the presence of the one in the midst of history, who calls upon us with the words: 'Follow me!'

That would mean that the ultimate secret of knowing is in following Jesus. When we accept that calling, we are not then people who pretend to know everything. But we know that we are on the way, that we are 'in via', that we have the clue that will lead us into the fullness of the truth.

Obviously there will be those who reply, 'This is irrational. This is a mere leap of faith. It doesn't have a rational basis.' But it is so easy to point out the illusion which underlies that criticism. If this world is ultimately a thing, if everything in this world, including ourselves, is ultimately to be understood in terms of physics, chemistry, mechanics and biology and in the last analysis this world is a thing, then the way to know would simply be by observation and reason.

But if the ultimate reality by which this world is constituted is personal, the eternal love of the triune God, then the only way by which we can come to know the truth is by a personal response to a personal calling. And that is what we affirm as Christians. The Bible states, 'The fear of the Lord is the beginning of wisdom' (Proverbs 9:10). It does not say, 'The fear of the Lord is the beginning of religious education.' It is the beginning of *all* wisdom and this is the clue by which, in the end, we shall understand all things. It also means we have to remind our contemporaries that there is no spectators' gallery.

When that young man told me, 'Well, of course, that's just what you think,' he was typically representing the illusion that there is available to us some kind of so-called objective standpoint where things are not just what you *think* but somehow stand apart from any thinking. This is an illusion. We are in fact called upon to a personal commitment, to understanding and knowing, and the limits of natural theology are at that point.

It is only because we know that God has revealed himself in the grace of our Lord Jesus Christ in the actual flesh and blood of his incarnation, death and resurrection that we are able to recognise the illusion of Descartes. Consequently, we accept our calling to be among those who follow the word addressed to us by the incarnate Lord, and know that this is the way to the truth.

CHAPTER TWO

Authority

Scripture, Tradition, Reason, Experience

On the whole we regard authority as a bad thing. Our culture developed in revolt against external authority. One of the great themes of the eighteenth century Age of Reason, from which our modern world was largely born, was that of freedom from external authority and the affirmation that true authority must be internal. Individual freedom of thought, freedom of conscience and self-responsibility in finding out the truth – these were the ideas that prevailed.

But freedom of thought cannot be the last word. This is because there is a real world out there and we have to find out about it and discover whether we are right or wrong in what we think. So that these freedoms – freedom of conscience and freedom of thought – though they are the absolutely sacred icons of our culture, they cannot have, or be, the last word unless we are to substitute virtual reality for the real thing. And we cannot live unceasingly in virtual reality.

We know this in the most practical of ways. We know that a teacher explaining perhaps a theory in geometry, or a poem, will exercise a certain authority in saying to the children, 'Look, this is true and I want you to understand this.' And the children might, to begin with, simply accept what is taught on the authority of the teacher. But, of course, the teacher will not be satisfied if the only answer they can give for the truth of a theory is that their teacher said so. The competent teacher will not be satisfied until the child has seen for himself or herself that what has been taught is true. So in this way, authority is both external and internal.

The woman at the well of Samaria told the people of her village about her experience of Jesus and they took her word. But it was only when they went and saw for themselves that they declared, 'Now we have heard for ourselves, and we know that this man really is the Saviour of the world' (John 4:42). Again, we see the internal and external sides of authority.

Let us begin by discussing the external side of authority. Take the question: 'What are the external authorities for what we believe as Christians?' I suppose a typical Protestant answer might be: 'The Bible'. A typical Roman Catholic answer would be: 'The Bible and tradition'. And there is a long tradition in Anglican theology which says: 'Bible, tradition, reason'.

Let us look first at the Catholic answer, for there is much to be said for it. In a certain sense one can say that the Bible, or at least the New Testament, is subsequent to the church.

When St Paul was writing the letters which form a great part of our New Testament, there was no Bible, at least no New Testament. There was the Bible as those people knew it, what we call the Old Testament, but the apostles themselves were reporting a tradition.

Paul was very careful to say over and again, 'I am handing on to you what I received.' The Latin words are the words which in English become 'tradition': the handing over of what is received.

In the first sermon of Peter, after the day of Pentecost, there is an outline of the story. In 1 Corinthians 15:1 St Paul writes, 'I delivered to you,' and the word he uses is 'tradition'. What he had received he transmitted to them in the form of 'tradition' – that Christ died, according to the Scriptures, and was buried and rose from the dead and was then seen by so many people. So it was the apostles who created what we call the New Testament. In that sense the tradition is prior to the book. The apostles were not simply original thinkers, putting out their own ideas about theology. They were, on the contrary, passing on something given to them, given in the first instance, by word of mouth.

Paul, with the older apostles, Peter, James, John and Barnabas and so forth, was hearing that tradition. What we call the four Gospels have been formed by bringing together traditions that were treasured in the different churches of the early first century by those who had actually heard the words of Jesus and seen his deeds.

St Luke said in the introduction to his Gospel that he had made it his business to find out what the earliest witnesses had to say about Jesus: the relationship between the book and the community was two-way. In one sense it was the community which created the book, but in another sense it was the story they told which created the community and those two have always been reciprocally related to each other.

Those first apostles were always careful to affirm that what they were saying was the true interpretation of the Scriptures, namely the Old Testament. So that the coming of Jesus and the events of the gospel had made it possible, for the first time, to understand the real meaning of those prophecies and laws. Their true meaning had become manifest in the things concerning Jesus so that the heart of the tradition, which they received and carried forward, was that, according to the Scriptures, those things actually happened.

The final fixing of the canon of the New Testament, the decision about which books should or should not be included, was a church decision. Some books were the subject of long debate and doubt. It was only with great hesitation that the second book of Peter, for instance, was included in the canon. On the other hand, the gospel of Thomas, which claims to have been written by an apostle, was rejected. It was judged not to be a faithful representation of the tradition, and if we read the gospel of Thomas today we can see why that was deemed to be so.

In one sense the fixing of the text of our New Testament was a work of the church. But on the other hand, the very fact that the church in that way fixed the canon meant that the church recognised that it was not free to think whatever it wanted. Its thinking must forever be controlled by those writings which represent, with the greatest faithfulness, the authentic tradition concerning the original message relating to Jesus.

What then does it mean to speak of the Bible as the word of God? Let us begin by recognising that the phrase 'the word of God' is used in three respects in the New Testament. It is used first of Jesus himself, then of the preaching of the apostles and thirdly of the written Scriptures. The fundamental use of the phrase is with reference to Jesus himself: God, who in sundry times and various ways had spoken through the prophets, had now spoken through his Son. He was, as St John said, the 'Word made flesh', the Word present as a human life. And we cannot stress and emphasise that point enough.

In the previous chapter we looked at the effect upon all our thinking of the past three centuries, of the vision of truth propounded and advocated by Descartes. He saw the human mind as though it was a kind of disembodied eye. He took as the model of truth what was called an objective view where no subject was involved. The mind was outside of and apart from the observed. Descartes taught us to take as the ideal of truth a so-called objective truth, in which the subject was not involved.

In complete contrast to that, we have an actual man of history, living in a particular time and place, identified and personified as the Truth. So the truth is known in exact contradiction to Descartes. It is known in the first sense in the actual bodily reality of this man Jesus. He *is* the Word of

25

God. So the Word of God is not a detached or merely an intellectual or mental entity, but ultimately Jesus himself.

But then naturally, and secondly, the preaching of Jesus as Lord is described as 'preaching the Word'. The preaching of the apostles is the Word of God. And here again, it is not a detached or objective truth where no subject is involved. It is precisely the Word in action, the Word being engaged in the actual life of the world. So that is the second sense in which the phrase 'Word of God' is used.

The third sense occurs in the written testimony to God's word as given to us in Scriptures. The recorded writings of the apostles, the prophets and the books of the Old Testament are now understood as being testimony to this Word made manifest, made incarnate in Jesus Christ. So that all the writings we have in the Bible have been Scripture from the very beginning.

It is not the case, to put it bluntly, that there were certain writings which were canonised and came to be regarded as Scripture. It is rather that all of these writings – which are the record of actual involvement in the name of God with the life of the world – are from the very beginning part of the action of God in the world. There is no pre-scriptural phase, so to speak, of these writings.

So there are these three senses, of which the first is funda-mental: Jesus Christ, the Word of God; secondly, the preaching of Christ as Lord is the preaching of the Word; and thirdly, the realisation that the record of the testimony of the prophets and apostles in relation to Jesus is in fact the word of God.

For the first 1,400 years of the life of the church the Bible was essentially a book that was not read but heard. There was no printed Scripture. The Bible was known through the liturgy of the church and was read and expounded in church. It was part of the testimony of the church to Jesus Christ. But when printing was invented it created something new and different. It meant the Bible could now be read outside the church by an individual not involved in the actual worship of the church. It was still, of course, within the world of Christendom. It was still being read in the context of Christian faith, because that was the public faith of Europe. But it was liberated from the direct control of the church. It was a control which in many ways came eventually to obscure some of the essential teachings of the Scriptures. So it was read outside the church, but still within Christendom, and read as Scripture, as Holy Scripture.

Then we come to that great intellectual conversion of Europe, called by those who passed through it the Enlightenment or the Age of Reason, when the Bible began to be read, not as Scripture, but simply as a book – one of the many that were filling up the world. It was read, however, not within the tradition which controlled its creation, but within another tradition.

Perhaps the fundamental change that took place during that eighteenth century intellectual conversion, which created our modern understanding of the world, was the return to the ancient classical view that eternal truths transcended history. These truths were beyond history and were, so to speak, beyond time. These eternal or universal truths were such that history could only provide illustrations but could never form the basis or be the ground itself. One of the most quoted sayings of the Enlightenment came from the German philosopher, G. E. Lessing (1729–1781). He asserted: 'Accidental truths of history can never be the proof of necessary truths of reason.'

Sir Isaac Newton's life spanned the seventeenth and eighteenth century and his cosmology, envisioning the universe as a huge clock mechanism, which operates indefinitely, was perhaps one of the eternal truths of reason: it was timeless, not based upon any historical happening and – if you come to see it that way – just how things were. But, as the Bible is a story of happenings in history, one might find within it illustrations of eternal truths, but they cannot be the source of our knowledge of truth because – remember Descartes – truth is something known only as an objective reality. In other words, the mind contemplates the world from outside.

How was the church to respond to that position? Broadly speaking, there were two possibilities which we have come to call liberal and fundamentalist. I do not like these labels because they are so often used as an excuse for not listening to the other person – but they are helpful.

The liberal response was fundamentally an evangelical missionary reaction: how can we get the people of this modern world to listen to the Bible? How can we make the Bible intelligible to this modern age? This was what the liberal tried to answer. And the father of the whole liberal movement was the great German theologian, Friedrich Schleiermacher (1768–1834). He said that deeper than all the findings of science and metaphysics there was something fundamental in human nature which urged that we were all ultimately dependent upon God. We are not our own sovereigns.

Whatever our beliefs, we know at heart that we are dependent creatures. There is a sense of absolute dependence upon a greater reality. Schleiermacher sought to find a standing ground from which he could convince the rationalists of his time that the Bible had something to say.

Into our Christian thinking this blessed word 'experience' was launched, where religion became a matter of experience and of internal feelings. Until the nineteenth century, the English word 'experience' was used in the sense in which we now say 'experiment'. Its use in our modern sense came from Germany in the nineteenth century and has now become widely accepted. You do not ask: experience of what? It is just experience that came to be valued as the heart of religion and, of course, Christianity. But not uniquely of Christianity because all religions are full of religious experience. And so, the Bible came to be valued as a marvellous treasury of religious experience.

But then if you begin to ask about the truth of the Bible from the point of view of the enlightened modern world, then you begin to ask all those questions raised by what is called the 'historical critical' method. This method has dominated theological colleges and seminaries for the past hundred years or so. On examination it is found that the historical critical method is based upon a whole set of assumptions about what is possible. And on the basis of those assumptions – drawn from another source, not from the Bible – you decide how to understand the Bible and how much of it can be accepted.

The positive fruit of this movement is that there arose a serious and determined effort to disentangle the sources which have been brought together in the Bible, as we have it now, and to examine the various oral and written traditions that have been brought together in this book we call the Bible. But, as I have said, the essential heart of this whole response was how the message of the Bible could be made intelligible to the modern world. And it was in that sense a missionary intention.

It is only now that we can see it was the wrong reaction. The question to the world should have been put the other way round: 'How can the world make any sense at all without the gospel?' But perhaps it would have been too difficult, in the wake of the triumphant Age of Reason, to see that this was the real question.

The other response is the one labelled fundamentalist, also shaped by the Enlightenment. Indeed, it is impossible to live in this modern world without being moulded and influenced to a great extent by the Enlightenment. The fundamentalist response takes the form that if the Bible is the word of God, then it must have that kind of certitude which Descartes has taught us to regard as the bench mark of truth. And so it must be affirmed that the Bible is verbally inerrant in every statement and that it possesses that kind of objective certainty which Descartes regarded as the only real knowledge. This means we are imposing upon the Scriptures a concept of truth foreign to them.

To use a simple illustration. When St Paul wrote to the Corinthians, 'I thank God that I baptised none of you – oh yes, I baptised Crispus and Gaius, and the household of Stephanus, but I don't remember who else' (1 Corinthians 1:14–16 paraphrased), he was obviously not writing a kind of inerrant text to satisfy Descartes. It was a different kind of language. And to impose upon it a concept of certitude that has arisen from a particular philosophical tradition is to do injustice and even violence to the Scriptures.

If we want to know what the word of God is, we must not begin by first deciding what it is or what it must be, and then imposing that view upon the Scriptures. We have to find out from the Scriptures themselves what the word of God is, how God speaks to us. And the fundamental mistake is to forget the great insight of the Reformation – that our knowledge of God is by grace through faith.

Our knowledge of God is not the kind of thing that Descartes was advocating. It is a knowledge that comes through atonement, reconciliation and forgiveness. It comes through the gracious action of God addressed to us as human beings who need to repent and be converted. It is a different kind of understanding of truth, and that is the fundamental point to which we must cling.

Look at the Anglican triad: Scripture, tradition, reason. One can understand the inclusion of reason because we have to use our reason in reading the Bible as in anything else. But the point is that reason is not an independent source of information about what is the case. Reason is the faculty by which we make sense of the material and data that is given.

All rational discourse has two characteristics. First of all, something has to be taken for granted. There has to be some data, something given. Secondly, rational discourse always operates within a tradition, which in turn implies language. Reason cannot operate without a language and languages are different. Language cannot operate effectively without a variety of symbols, concepts and models. No reasoning can take place without information, a tradition, and language. In this context language goes beyond mere communication, or the signalling of wants or desires – the type of communication available to animals – and enters the realm of categorising and symbolising reality, which in turn enables reasoning to take place.

The Christian use of reason is that exercise which takes as the data, as the given, the fact of the gospel. The gospel takes the incarnation, death and resurrection of Jesus Christ as what is given. We should not try to go behind it, for it is the starting point. It operates within the tradition of Christian belief which has developed from that beginning.

But if reason is invoked in the sense in which I am afraid it has often been, it is really reason based upon the tradition that stems from the Enlightenment. This takes as the fundamental data simply the facts available for empirical observation by the methods of modern science in the modern world. So that one tradition is brought into play as the critique of another. It is not the independent exercise of reason.

One of the most famous philosophical works of the Enlightenment was Immanuel Kant's *Religion Within the Limits of Reason Alone*. For Kant it was reason, as he understood it, which provided the basic tradition and religion must be acceptable only as it fits into that tradition. Nicholas Wolterstorff, a modern philosopher, has written an excellent little book called *Reason Within the Limits of Religion Alone* and the writer points out that all reasoning takes place within a tradition of reasoning and that for most of human history it has been religion that has provided the tradition within which reason works.

In the world of Islam the Koran is understood to be the actual verbatim dictation by God in the Arabic language and to be accepted, whether you understand it or not, simply as God's revelation of the truth. And because all translation means interpretation – since you cannot translate something without at least trying to understand it – and since human understanding is always fallible, it is therefore an article of faith in Islam that the Koran cannot be translated.

If you pick up an English version of the Koran you will notice that it is called 'an interpretation of the Koran' never 'a translation'. In order to actually hear God's word you must learn Arabic but even then you are not expected to understand, though you may try, but it is not expected. It is a purely external authority and the ideal of Islam is that one should be able to recite the entire Koran in Arabic.

By contrast, we look at Jesus because the parallel is not Koran and Bible, but Koran and Jesus. It is Jesus who is the Word of God in the primary and fundamental sense and Jesus, as we know, did not write a book. The only knowledge we have of his writing is when he wrote in the dust when a woman was charged with adultery. Jesus could have written a book but he did not. He gathered a company of disciples and he called them 'friends'. He told them: 'I do not call you servants because a servant does not understand what his master is doing. I have called you friends, for everything that I have heard from my father, I have made known to you' (John 15:15).

What we find in the Gospels is exactly what I have been trying to describe: an apprenticeship to a tradition. Jesus took his disciples as apprentices and, as we know, apprenticeship means much more than reading a book. One cannot become a doctor simply by reading medical textbooks. There is no alternative to actually becoming an apprentice to a skilled doctor, watching the expert at work and following by example.

And so it was with Jesus. He did not issue a manual of instructions. He entrusted the revelation of God to this company of friends who were not simply slaves, but real friends, who were to understand what he was saying. And that is why we have different accounts of the words and deeds of Jesus in the four Gospels. We do not have any parable or miracle about which we can say we know exactly what Jesus said or did.

From Descartes' point of view we have no reliable certainty. This is the charge the Muslims make against Christians. If you have been in discussion with Muslims you will know that the fact that we have four Gospels, and not one, is used by them as an argument to prove that we have lost the original Gospel, the Injil, and that what we have is a series of botched attempts to recover it. But this is not something to regret; it is fundamental to our faith as this is the way God has made known his revelation to us.

There was an attempt in the early Syriac church to overcome this difficulty by combining the four Gospels into a single narrative, the *Diatessaron*, which comes from Greek and means 'through four', but the church rejected the idea. These four distinct Gospels were kept as they are, in true obedience to the intention of Jesus. This helps us to see what it means for God to reveal himself to us. It is precisely through this presence of the living man Jesus Christ, apprenticing a group of friends to learn and to follow, that God has chosen to reveal himself.

Now we come to the great thing which is absolutely central – the work of the Holy Spirit. It is only if we understand the Christian teaching about the Holy Spirit that we have the clue to overcoming this dichotomy between objective and subjective which has almost paralysed the thinking of our modern world.

First, according to the teaching of the apostles, we have

the work of the Spirit in communicating the word of God through the mouths of the prophets. It is by the work of the Spirit that they were enabled to communicate the word of God to their times. Then we have the great event of Pentecost which enabled the apostles to communicate the Word of God incarnate in Jesus to their contemporaries. It is by the power of the Spirit that they were enabled truly to interpret Jesus to the world around them.

Next we have the great passage in St John where Jesus, on the eve of his passion, said to his disciples, 'There are many things I have to tell you but you cannot bear them now' (John 16:12). There was a vast amount which that little company of Palestinian Jews in the first century could not know; they could not have a universal knowledge. There was much that they had to learn, but he told them, 'You cannot bear them now, but the Spirit of truth when he comes, he will guide you into the truth as a whole . . . for he will take what is mine and show it to you. All that the Father has is mine; therefore I said that he will take what is mine and show it to you' (John 16:12–15).

In one sense there has been a full revelation: 'He who has seen me has seen the Father,' said Jesus (John 14:9b). So, in one sense, it was a full revelation and yet there was a vast amount to be learnt. And in the New Testament itself we see the disciples beginning to learn and, led by the Spirit, to start going beyond what Jesus had said, for example, in the matter of circumcision.

The work of the Spirit cannot be separated from the name

of Jesus. As St Paul and St John said, the test that it was truly the Holy Spirit was that it led to the confession of Jesus as Lord. So the Spirit is not something, as it were, that goes beyond Jesus, but the Spirit illuminates the world in the light of the revelation in Jesus Christ.

It often is said that this makes us sectarian. And if people say, 'But the Spirit's work is much wider than this talk about Jesus,' the answer is, 'All that the Father has is mine' – so the name of Jesus is not a sectarian name. Everything that exists belongs to Jesus. And it is the work of the Spirit through the church down the ages – as the church moves into new continents, new generations and new cultures – to illuminate the world in the light of Jesus Christ so that the truth, the truth in all its fullness, is seen to be present in Jesus Christ.

So in this way this objective-subjective divide is healed. There is the objective given reality of Jesus Christ: this man of Nazareth who belonged both to a particular time in history and to a specific human culture. He was not part of Chinese or African culture and nor was he part of the twentieth century. His life was an objective fact and we may study him as we listen to the Scriptures, and seek to understand them. There is at the same time this working of the Holy Spirit in our hearts which enables Jesus to illuminate the whole of our experience as we move onwards through the history of the world and across all nations and cultures.

I find the Eastern Orthodox way of putting this most helpful, because they say that the Word and the Spirit are the two hands of the Father. The Word – Jesus in the flesh –

and the Spirit – universal, everywhere, present in all ages and times – are the two hands of the one Father. They are not two different things. And this is one more place where the doctrine of the Trinity is not a puzzle, but the solution to a puzzle, because there is no other ultimate solution to this dichotomy between subjective and objective.

How in practice do we read the Bible? I think we can waste a lot of time talking about our doctrine of Scripture when what is important is the practice of how we actually treat them. We first need to recognise that as we read the Scriptures we are apprentices to a tradition and have much to learn.

It is not that we should simply take it as a Muslim takes the Koran, whether we understand it or not. We should open our hearts and minds to what is given and seek in our total daily life to grasp more fully what it means. The external authority is there but our task is to internalise it and understand it and not to pretend that we understand all of it – or even that we can accept it all. Our business is to allow it to shape our thinking and practice so that we see ourselves as apprentices in this great tradition, of which the Bible is the central clue.

All of this must be tackled in the context of actual discipleship because there can be no apprenticeship which involves the mere reading of a book. It must be worked at against a background of worship, obedience and discipleship. One result of the Enlightenment is that the Bible has been taken out of the church and perhaps lodged too much in the universities and schools for academic study. Of course, it is perfectly legitimate to study the Bible in academic institutions. The universities may help us with all kinds of insights, and thank God for that. But the real understanding of the Bible can only be in church, in the context of worship and obedience and in connection with the tradition of all the saints who sought to be faithful, in their own day, to the teaching of the Bible.

We have to use our reason in reading the Bible. But it is a reason which is based not upon some other tradition but on the tradition of the Bible itself. Obviously, when we read the Bible there are great tensions. Put the book of Joshua alongside the Sermon on the Mount and you have a mind-blowing contradiction. In many other places, there are further tensions. Take, for example, the passages on justification by faith written by St Paul and those written by St James. Consider the nature of the state in Revelation 13 and in Romans 13: in Romans, the Roman Empire is the power ordained by God while in Revelation it is the beast out of the Abyss.

How do we cope with them? How do we deal with these tensions? The ultimate clue is in Jesus himself. We must recognise that in the Bible God is leading a people to a deeper understanding of his nature and that we therefore have to read the Bible in this light. When Jesus begins a statement with the words, 'You have been told in old times, but I say unto you', this is not an absolute discontinuity. Jesus is instead bringing an old commandment to its full strength and deeper understanding in his own teaching.

We have to recognise that in the Bible we have the story

of God leading a people into an ever deepening under-standing. That means that we have to read every text in the context of the gospel itself, for it is the clue to our under-standing of Scripture.

It means that we read every text in its cultural context. Let me give another simple illustration. It is said that St Paul accepted slavery and therefore we cannot trust him. But slavery was an integral part of his culture and you cannot simply jump out of your society or your time. The Bible forbids usury – the taking of interest on loans. In modern usage usury means the charging of iniquitous rates of interest, but the charging of reasonable rates is nevertheless integral to our own present economic system. We know that the Bible forbids it yet we all practise it. We cannot leap out of our society. Paul could not suddenly propel himself out of the first century society in which he lived, but he was able to plant the seeds of change. When Paul considered the case of the runaway slave Onesimus he did not tell him to go under-ground and become a fugitive. Instead, he sent him back to his master, but with a new status. This was the status of a representative of the apostles in the house of Philemon.

Paul thus introduced into that existing institution of slavery something which would eventually transform it. This simple illustration is true in many other cases. We must always read any text in the context of the culture of its time. So in reading the Scriptures we should try to understand their direction, and the meaning to which the texts point, in relation to their place and time.

But the ultimate tension in the Bible, which causes us discomfort, is that straining between the holy wrath of God and the holy love of God – a tension which lies at the very heart of the being of God. And that is a tension which within this life we will never fully overcome. We have to take with the greatest seriousness both those passages of Scripture which speak of the holy wrath of God, his rejection of sin in every form, and those passages which speak of the all-inclusive and utterly forgiving love of God for the sinner. In our human strength we cannot hold that tension but it is in the atoning work of Jesus Christ, in that cross which is both the judgment and the salvation of the world, that the clue lies by which we can grasp these tremendous tensions within the Scriptures.

We must allow the Scriptures to shape our minds and teach us how God speaks to us, what it means to speak of the Word of God. We must allow the Scriptures to play such a vast part in our lives that we think in terms of the horizon that Scripture gives us. It is in the light of the Scriptures as a whole that we eventually come to understand our own lives. We come to understand who we really are, rather than avoiding who we are. We realise where we have come from and where we are going, and what choices are available to us on the way. It is only when we discover how to live in this manner that we learn what it really means to speak of Scripture as being the word of God.

CHAPTER THREE

Creation

Things Visible and Invisible

'In the beginning God created the heavens and the earth' (Genesis 1:1). This was the absolute beginning. Before that, there was neither space nor time, nothing at all. It was the complete and total origin of all things: 'In the beginning, God.'

In Colossians 1:16 St Paul makes this more explicit: ' . . . all things were created: things in heaven and on earth, visible and invisible.' That is an important clarification of what is intended by the words 'heaven' and 'earth' – both the visible and invisible. If we had kept that firmly and consistently in mind I think perhaps some of the futile arguments that have gone on in the past among theologians might have been avoided.

For example, there have been prolonged arguments and disputes about whether something was right because God commanded it, or whether God commanded it because it was right. To advance that idea implies that there is something called 'right' which existed, as it were, before God or exists apart from God. The thinking that is intrinsic to the phrase 'all things invisible' protects us from this notion. We think of concepts such as right and wrong, beauty or coherence, as though they possess a kind of timeless existence, but this is not so. All things visible and invisible in heaven and on earth have their sole origin in God's mighty word.

If we could only adopt the attitude enshrined in that famous little notice that Harry S. Truman placed on his desk in 1945 when he was President of the United States: 'The buck stops here.' He assumed responsibility for things he would not pass on to someone else. In a sense, in all our intellectual inquiries, we need to have that little motto in front of us. Here is where the final questioning stops and we have to humbly accept the answer.

I want to discuss five points that flow from those first chapters of Genesis about God's creation. The first is that there is an emphasis on distinguishing and separating things one from another: light from darkness, sea from land, the different species of animals and plants, the distinctness and specificity of everything that has been created.

The second point is the fact that the created world has been given a sort of autonomy. It has a life of its own. Plants, animals and humans are able to reproduce their own species. The created world has a being, a life and a movement of its own. This creation is not just a kind of extension of God or an emanation from him, but distinct from him. It was so clear-cut and well-defined that on the seventh day God could rest. The creation went on. God did not have to keep pushing it along all the time. He could rest and contemplate his creation and, as we shall see, that is a very important point for practical discipleship.

The third aspect is that the whole world was brought into existence as a home for the human family. The purpose and meaning of it all was that it should be such a home. I think perhaps this emerges most strikingly in what is said about the creation on the fourth day: the creation of the sun, moon and stars. These words were almost certainly written during the time when the people of Israel were enslaved under the mighty Babylonian Empire, working in powerless bondage under the shadows of those enormous temples and palaces that we know existed in Babylon.

For the Babylonians – like so many other cultures in the world – the sun, moon and stars were gods. They were supernatural heavenly bodies, divine entities to be worshipped and prayed to. But here our text says this was not so. They were lamps placed in the sky for the home that God had made for his family. The whole meaning of the creation was that it was to be a home for God's family.

The fourth thing to be grasped is that the human family has been given a particular responsibility, and that is to cherish the creation. It has been given a delegated responsibility from the Creator to bring the creation into the perfection which the Creator desires. And this in itself is an important message in relation to all our ecological fears of the present time. It was not God's intention that the world should become a wilderness. It was to be a garden for the human family to nourish and cultivate.

Humankind was granted responsibility for the naming and classifying of animals so that there was from the onset a relationship with them. The Christian scholar C.S. Lewis suggested in one of his books that it was part of our responsibility as human beings to do all we could to bring animals to the fullness of their potential. Take, for example, a faithful dog. One thinks of those marvellous animals used by shepherds on the Cheviot Hills in northern England. Such dogs are incredibly intelligent and responsive, and if you contrast them with a wild creature like a fox or a wolf, you then begin to realise what God intended human beings to do in relation to the potential of animal existence. We are given a delegated responsibility to bring the whole created world into that perfection for which God made it.

My fifth point is that God looked each day at everything he had made and saw that it was good. This is a wonderful phrase, and it is repeated after each day of creation until it culminates, on the sixth day, with God's affirmation that all he has made is 'very good' (Genesis 1:31). This phrase contrasts sharply with so much of human religion which has often regarded the world as a bad and dangerous place, a place of darkness. The Christian reformer John Calvin, in a wonderful description, considered the world to be 'a theatre for God's glory' – a place where his glory was reflected in the created world.

If we compare this with pagan views of the created world, we see how great the difference is. I am, of course, using language rather loosely here because 'pagan' is a word of broad meaning. It includes an immense variety of different beliefs, but there are certain common things, which are fairly widespread in the world, which pagan views share. For example, there is the idea that nature itself is in some way divine and that it is the ultimate reality. This is expressed in primitive animistic forms where trees and rivers and mountain tops are seen as places where divine energies rest. It can also be seen very clearly in many forms of Hinduism where the powers of nature are identified with God.

If, for example, you go to a Sivaite temple you will see in the central shrine a phallus, a symbol of the potency of human sexuality, and guarding the door a bull, the supreme symbol of pure animal power. Those sheer powers of nature are seen as divine and as the ultimate reality.

Alternatively, and these two things can go together, nature is seen to be transient. All natural things die and pass away – except things like mountains – but even these eventually erode. Most of nature is marked by transience. The plants blossom, grow, and then fade and die, as do human beings and animals. So throughout human history there has been a strong tendency to feel that ultimate reality is beyond nature, that it must be something transhistorical, eternal. It is something to be grasped by the mind, rather than these fleeting things that we know by our rather inadequate senses of sight, feeling and hearing.

This was clear in the classical world into which the Christian church was first launched. According to Plato, the ultimate realities were ideas and non-material things. All the different things in this world were shadowy or imperfect representations of a perfect reality that existed in an invisible world of ideas. Or, according to Aristotle, a sharp distinction existed between 'substance' and what he referred to as 'accidents'. What we see, hear, touch and feel are the accidents of things. But the real substance, what lies behind those accidents, is something we can never know.

There was a sharp distinction between what the Greeks called the sensible world and the intelligible world. The sensible world was grasped by the five senses of sight, smell, hearing, taste and touch. On the other hand, the intelligible world is that which we apprehend or perceive with the mind, or perhaps contemplate with the spirit. So the way to ultimate reality was to bypass the material things of the visible world, and to bypass those accidental happenings in history which cannot give us ultimate truth, and to press on beyond them. To pass through this visible world to an eternal invisible world beyond would be achieved by the powers of human reason or mystical contemplation, self-transcendence and all the various techniques of yoga.

By implication history could not have any real significance. History might appear to be linear and moving onwards, but this was an illusion. It was really just going round in circles and everything that had happened would happen again. Our understanding of history would therefore be modelled on our perception of nature as a perpetual cycle of growth, development, maturity, decay and death, followed by new growth – and so on. So the actual happenings of history could have no ultimate significance.

Those were the dominant ideas of the pagan world into

which the Christian gospel was projected. During the period when Christianity was a persecuted minority religion struggling for its life and winning its way by the testimony of its martyrs, there could be no mature discussion between those who stood for the Christian gospel and those who held these pagan views. But once Christianity was acknowledged as a permitted religion, and eventually as the religion of the Empire, the way was opened for vigorous discussion. This occurred especially in the great intellectual centre of Alexandria, the greatest in the world at that time, with its tremendous library. And in the fourth and fifth centuries many vigorous intellectual discussions took place between Christian thinkers and the practitioners of science and philosophy.

Those early Christian theologians learned from these discussions that nothing could be built on classical philosophy. The gospel provided a completely new starting point. If the Logos, the divine reason for the existence of all things – by which they were made and for which they existed – had actually appeared in human history in the person of Jesus Christ, then that had to be the starting point of all our thinking. From that standpoint it was then possible to step back from the dominant classical worldview and pose some specific questions from which certain principles emerged which ever since have defined and determined the development of European thought.

The first principle is that since the world is the creation of a rational God, and since God has created us in his image, then a rationality prevails which is within the grasp of reason.

We can therefore take it as a matter of faith that in principle the universe is ultimately comprehensible, though there may be many things that we do not yet understand. And that is the indispensable foundation upon which modern science has been built.

If the universe was a place where all kinds of demons and spirits could perform their arbitrary deeds according to whim and fancy, then there could be no certainty of the existence of a rational universe. Why do European scientists take it for granted – unlike the thinking in many other parts of the world – that if two similar experiments are conducted in two different places with dissimilar results, then there must be a mistake? The passionate conviction that these things cannot be totally irreconcilable, that one must be able to find some pattern of thought which will enable us, coherently, to hold these things together, is what has made possible the enormous advance of science.

This has one particular illustration with regard to the so-called heavenly bodies. In pagan thought, most certainly in the thought of Aristotle which dominated the science of the first centuries, the sun, moon and stars were heavenly bodies. They were not made of the same four elements of earth, air, fire and water of which this world was made, but were of a different kind of being. The Christian theologians declared, 'No. Since God created them all, they are all of the same kind.' One of the ironies of the history of thought is that when the controversial physicist and astronomer Galilei Galileo (1564–1642) got to work with his telescope and con-

49

cluded that the moon was made of the same stuff as earth, he was roundly condemned by the church because the church, earlier in the twelfth century, had taken Aristotle on board again. That is one of the many ironies in the history of the relation between science and religion.

Since creation is not an emanation, this created world has a relative autonomy but it is not an absolute autonomy. The world has a measure of independence which does not depend for its continuing existence on God constantly causing all things to happen. In the thought of Aristotle – and here he is followed by Islam to this day – everything that moved was governed by God. The stars move because God is moving them. The concept of momentum was wholly foreign to classical thought.

If I throw a ball into the air, we now take it for granted that in the absence of gravity it will go on moving with its own momentum gained from that initial thrust. But that was a concept unknown to the classical world. If the ball went on moving, it was because God was pushing it along. It was the rediscovery of the concept of momentum in the Middle Ages that made possible the revolutionary physics and mathematics of Sir Isaac Newton. This is one example of the way those early theologians challenged the prevailing worldview and insisted that this world, since it was a creation, had a relative independence. Everything that happened was not the direct action of God.

But the great and difficult question to which we must return is this: 'How much autonomy does the world have?' It is possible to go to one extreme and suggest that it has almost complete autonomy. This is the image of the world as a clock which functions perfectly without the clock-maker's interference. If the clock-maker was highly skilled, having made the clock and wound it up, there would be no need for further interference.

That way of looking at the world, which is called deism, the belief in a creator who did not intervene in the universe, was a dominant view in the seventeenth century when Newton was working. Although Newton's theology was deist, he nevertheless believed that the 'clock' needed occasional adjustment and that God would do this if and when it became necessary.

But it was not long before the clock-maker was made redundant. With the approach of the nineteenth century the view emerged where the dominant picture of the world was seen as a pure mechanism which worked without reference to any divine purpose and from which anything that we might call the supernatural, had been banished.

There is a well-known story of the famous physicist and astronomer Pierre-Simon La Place (1749–1827) who produced a great work on astronomy that contradicted Newton's worry that perturbations in planetary orbits would lead to long-term instability of the solar system. He presented it to Napoleon, who after reading it, said, 'But, Monsieur La Place, I do not see any reference to God in this work.' To which La Place replied, 'I have no need of that hypothesis.' (Newton thought that divine intervention was necessary to ensure stability.) The reply of La Place could be a motto for nineteenth century science which still has such a large influence in our own time. It depicts a world so totally independent that the very idea of God becomes unnecessary.

The other extreme, pantheism, perceives the world as being completely dependent on God at all times. God is in everything and doing everything, permanently pervading the universe so that you cannot, as it were, distinguish God from the world. God is immanent and cannot be distinguished from the world.

The post-Renaissance Dutch Jewish philosopher Baruch Spinoza (1632–1677) coined the widely used phrase *Deus sive Natura* – 'God, though equally it is Nature.' God was identified with nature because he impregnated and saturated the whole world. That way of thinking had reasserted itself around the time of the Renaissance because of the growing influence of Platonism.

So the Christian theologian has always had to find a way between those two extremes: deism, which makes the world so independent of God that there is no need for God, and pantheism, where God disappears into the world. Contemporary examples of this pantheistic way of thinking are the New Age movement and the so-called creation spirituality espoused by Dr Matthew Fox and the University of Creation Spirituality in California, USA.

Because of the incarnation, it is permissible to speak in terms of material means for our salvation. Let me explain what I mean. The Greeks developed the science and practice of medicine to a considerable degree, but the Hebrews rejected it. In the Old Testament there was no place for doctors. Healing was the direct work of God, the answer to prayer; it was part of forgiveness and because of this there was no place for medicine.

But the early Christian theologians argued that because God had used in the incarnation the actual material life of Jesus Christ to bring about the salvation of the world, consequently the use of material things for God's purposes of healing and salvation, could not be rejected. So in contrast to the Hebrews the Christians accepted and took advantage of Greek techniques and achievements in medicine. From this they developed the whole ethos of the healing ministry which since then has always been such an integral part of the church's work.

On that basis, of course, much greater and wider developments occurred. What we now call technology emerged, as well as all the different ways that material things have been developed to further human welfare. The great apostle of this movement was Francis Bacon, the Renaissance philosopher, who passionately believed that it was essential to develop science in order to improve and elevate the human race. In that respect we know how much has been accomplished, but we also know, sadly, how technology can become a terrible instrument in the cause of evil.

How is this question of autonomy to be answered? We have seen the two extremes. On the one hand deism teaches that the world carries on by itself without interference. On the other hand pantheism sees the world pervaded by God and that everything that happens in it is his work. How do we navigate the correct course between them? How is the created world related to God? That is perhaps one of the most difficult and inescapable problems in all Christian thinking about the world. At one end of the scale, and it comes in different forms, you could say there is no relationship. Or to put it the other way, the world has no independence at all. As I have said, Islam, following the Aristotelian tradition, is a religion whose adherents believe that everything that happens in the world is the direct action of God. The movement of a star or even a single stone is the direct action of God. And in that Islam follows the Aristotelian doctrine of the prime mover. Perhaps one of the most disturbing things to have happened in the course of Christian history was St Thomas Aquinas' attempt to synthesise biblical faith and this Aristotelian–Islamic rationalism. In this he came dangerously close to equating the God of the Bible with Allah – the prime mover of Aristotle and Islam – and I think even today we are still troubled by this confusion.

The reason why Islam rejects the central Christian doctrine of the crucifixion – that the Son of God died on the cross for our salvation – as simply impossible is because the Muslim world believes that Jesus was an apostle of God, and that God could not, and would not, have killed his own apostle. And since everything that happens in the world is the direct action of God, it would be incredible, impossible, indeed blasphemous, to hold the belief that Jesus died on the cross.

54

But the other extreme is to claim total autonomy for the world, to see it as a closed system controlled entirely by cause and effect. In the often repeated assertion of nineteenth century positivism, all causes were adequate to the effects they produced and all effects could be explained by the causes which produced them. Here there is no place for the supernatural. The way the world functions and is to be understood is entirely in terms of its own internal rules of action, or laws.

We can neither ask God to interfere in a world which is independent of him, nor on the other hand if the world is completely dependent on him can we ask God to change his mind to suit our wishes. In both cases prayer, intercession, miracles or divine providence – the belief that God rules over all things for the good of those who love him – become impossible.

I do not think that there is what could be called a metaphysical solution to this problem. I think it has to be, as in everything else, a solution that depends on faith in God's grace as revealed to us in the Bible.

There is first an orderliness, a pattern, a regularity which God has built into the created world. Genesis speaks of the regularity of the seasons, of day and night, summer and winter, spring time and harvest. God does not act arbitrarily and unpredictably. This orderliness has been made clear in the unravelling by science of the laws and regularities of nature, without which human freedom would be impossible.

We can only act responsibly if we know that the world is not an arbitrary place. If we do not know whether water will boil or freeze under heat then we could not make a cup of tea. All human freedom of thought and action depends upon the regularity God has given to the natural world. It relies upon the fact that God is consistent and not arbitrary or whimsical, that the world is not under the control of capricious little demons and imps who can play havoc with things. This given regularity of the world is the condition upon which our freedom is based.

Next there is human responsibility, and therefore the freedom to obey God. The Old Testament makes it absolutely clear that people are responsible before God. They can sin and repent. God makes them responsible for their actions, so that everything that happens is without doubt not the direct will of God. He has created a world where people possess the freedom to disobey him and act against his will.

Then – and this is a different kind of argument altogether – in our understanding of the regularities of the world, we have to recognise a hierarchy of logical levels. As we saw in Chapter 1, the simplest example would be to take a machine. You can understand a machine on one level in terms of its physical components and mechanical structure. You could understand completely the relationship between cause and effect which makes that machine work, but that does not begin to tell you its purpose – what the machine is for. Either the designer of the machine, or someone who has learned from its designer, must tell you. The question of the purpose of the machine is on a different logical level.

There is a whole hierarchy of levels: atomic, molecular,

mechanical, biological and so forth. Biology cannot be replaced by physics or mechanics. Chemistry cannot be replaced by physics and so on. And in particular, when we think about human behaviour, we know that from one point of view, at one logical level, it can be fully explained by the mechanical structure of the skeleton and the nerve impulses that move muscles and by the electrical activity in the brain which can be studied by a neurologist.

But none of this explains human motivation or purpose. This again is on a different logical level. We can therefore accept that while in one sense the world can be explained as a self-operating mechanism, it is not the total explanation. To attempt to understand the world, divorced from the purpose of the one who created it, is a logical mistake. It is to misunderstand the difference between logical levels. But it still remains a mystery why God has given us this freedom of choice to disobey him and has given to the world this regularity we cannot ignore or reject, and yet God, in the words of St Paul, 'works for the good of those who love him . . .' (Romans 8:28).

It is only by grace through faith that we can understand that. This awareness and insight begins with the cross and resurrection of Jesus. The cross of Jesus is, from one point of view, the most complete contradiction of God's purpose and yet has become, through his workings, the most complete expression in action of his purpose. The cross and resurrection of Jesus are the place where, by faith and in response to grace, we can believe. We can believe even if we cannot completely explain that despite the relative independence God has given the world, he nevertheless overrules all things for the good of those who love him.

Remember Plato's famous conundrum: 'What does it mean to seek the truth? If we know what truth is, why do we seek it? If we do not know what it is, how will we recognise it when we find it?' Plato's answer was in terms of the doctrine of reincarnation, that when we recognise truth it is because we have remembered something from a previous birth. Few people today accept that.

How do we understand? How can we answer Plato's conundrum? The answer surely involves heuristic passion to which I referred to in Chapter 1. This passion to know leaves us unwilling to accept mere confusion. It drives us to seek pattern, order, beauty and coherence in the multitude of things that face us. This could be a jumble of patterns on a page or the total perplexity of our very lives. It is not something which simply arises from below but is the response to the grace of God who, as St Paul says, 'has made us so that we might feel after him and find him'.

If all this is true then it brings all our knowing and being together, because we would then have to understand that it is the same grace of God calling all creation to its full potential, to completeness and perfection. It also explains the specific ways of nature where an acorn grows by these natural and consistent laws into an oak tree and not into a cabbage. It explains the evolution of living creatures in the world as the response of creation to the calling of its Creator and not, as

Darwin theorised, by blind forces from below. As human beings we possess an innate ability to make that response conscious. So with all our thoughts and feelings we are able to struggle to try to grasp the meaning of this wonderful and often perplexing world in which God has placed us. If that is the correct way of comprehending then we can understand the Fall because we know that the human story is not simply that of our faithful search for the truth and of our growth towards God's purpose.

If this picture is true then we can understand the Fall exactly as it is portrayed in Genesis 3 as the struggle to know perverted into a desire for personal power. The temptation of the serpent was not to trust God's word but to find out for oneself, so that we would be like God and we would know, not by faith but by knowledge. We would know as God knows. We would no longer innocently believe or trust but would actually *know* good and evil. The turning inwards of the longing for truth, into the self, is the essence of the Fall, and that is why our marvellous achievements in technology in using the powers of nature to serve humanity, have become for us a double-edged sword, for technology may also be used as a terrible instrument of evil.

Finally, as well as the visible world, we must remember that God made all things visible and invisible. Consider again Paul's words in Colossians 1:15–20. Look particularly at the words: 'For by him all things were created: things in heaven and on earth, visible and invisible . . .' – which we repeat in the creed. Paul then spells it out by talking of dominions or principalities. He is talking of power and authority, invisible things, which are nevertheless real and powerful. What does he mean?

We know from the rest of his letters what Paul was talking about because he makes use of this language in many places. Sometimes this language refers to the imperial power, the ultimate political power represented by Caesar in Romans 13. Sometimes it is the Jewish Law in Galatians. Elsewhere it is Greek philosophy in Colossians 2. Sometimes it is the whole establishment that put Jesus on the cross. In 1 Corinthians 2:8 he declares that if the principalities and powers had recognised Jesus they would never have crucified him. And those principalities and powers were represented by the Jewish priests, the scribes, the Pharisees, Pontius Pilate and the mob-like crowd bellowing and shouting for his death.

In every case those powers were represented by something visible. Caesar was a visible human being, but he was not just that; he was the present embodiment of a power that was there long before he was born and would be there long after he was dead.

There exist powers, ideologies, spiritual realities which are represented temporarily in human beings and their institutions but which also have a strange or curious existence of their own. This separate existence is enormously strong. I have become keenly aware of this from talking to such people as industrialists and bankers. From a human point of view these people seem to hold tremendous power but when you talk to them on a personal level they confess that they feel powerless. They feel trapped and helpless in the grip of a vast system which has a life of its own, operating and organising things from which they cannot free themselves. Nationalism, especially when represented in extreme forms, such as Nazism, is a particular example of these intangible forces.

Paul said that such powers were also created by God in Christ for a good and valid purpose because positive intentions and aspirations were found in such things as political authority and economic order. But unfortunately they have become fallen powers, part of this fallen creation. They have sought to absolutise themselves, to confer upon themselves powers which belong only to God. They thus become agents of evil against which we must fight.

But as the New Testament constantly reminds us, in his dying on the cross, Jesus disarmed and dethroned those powers. 'Now is the time for judgment on this world; now the prince of this world will be driven out' (John 12:31). They were not destroyed; they were disarmed. Paul stated in 1 Corinthians (15:24–25) that Jesus must reign until all the powers of the enemy were brought under his feet, and then he would hand the kingdom to the Father.

We live in times when these powers, which still exist and threaten us, have nevertheless been robbed of their final authority. We can therefore do as Paul says: 'Put on the full armour of God . . . For our struggle is not against flesh and blood, but against the rulers, against the authorities, against the spiritual forces . . .' (Ephesians 6:11–12). Our fight is not against other human beings, but against these principalities and powers, these invisible realities which are nevertheless part of the created world, God's creation, a fallen creation, but ultimately redeemed and under the power of Christ.

And so we live by grace through faith in the confidence that God, who in the beginning created all things visible and invisible, will in the end reign in glory over all things and that the earth will indeed be 'the theatre of his glory'.

CHAPTER FOUR

Salvation

Fall, Sin, Redemption, Atonement, Justification

'**G**od saw all that he had made, and it was very good' (Genesis 1:31).

Thank God for that basic truth at the very beginning of our Bible. But regrettably, we also know that it is not the last word. There follows the story of what we call the Fall. As Christians we understand our world as a good creation which has 'fallen', and the human race as made in God's image and therefore 'good', but 'fallen' and in 'rebellion'. It is at this point at which we are very strongly criticised by our culture.

To call someone a sinner is the greatest sin one can commit, as Gandhi once suggested when he remarked, 'To call people sinners is to undermine their humanity.' Many of our contemporaries would say that people need to be encouraged and told that they have great dignity and worth, and to label them sinners is a deep offence against their humanity.

Certainly from the time of the Renaissance onwards, European culture has tried to take an optimistic view of human nature. At the beginning of the 1776 American Declaration of Independence there occurs that momentous 'self-evident' statement that all people are created equal with equal rights to life, liberty and the pursuit of happiness. This was truly a

63

great statement. And happiness was the glorious new buzzword of the eighteenth century.

In the Middle Ages people did not expect happiness on earth, only the first taste of it. They expected happiness to come at the end. But especially from the Renaissance onwards that idea of happiness coming only at the end was regarded as a form of sedition, a sort of treason against humanity. Human nature was good. Of course there were bad people, but basically human nature was good and the task was to tell people so and encourage them to believe it.

We all know about sin. We know it especially because we are able to recognise other people as being sinners. We pass judgment on others and we have a strong tendency to identify sin with particular groups. For example, in the 1945 celebrations on VE Day we were reminded of the appalling evil of Nazi Germany before and during the second world war. People thought then that this demonic evil must not, could not, and would not ever recur. But we know that evil of this nature is still going on in many parts of the world. It has happened in Bosnia and continues to occur just about everywhere else. There is no doubt at all that the Bible speaks of us as sinners, although as a matter of fact there are very few references to the Fall in the Old Testament, except at the beginning of Genesis.

What grounds do we have for talking of sin? It is there in Genesis 3, but ultimately all Christian doctrine has to be validated at the centre point of the gospel. This is the point of the incarnation, death, resurrection and the victorious

Ascension of Jesus Christ. To put it candidly and rather bluntly, we know we are sinners because of what happened on Good Friday. That is the ultimate ground for our affirming that as a whole we are all sinners.

To use an illustration, I once had an experience that was meaningful to me: I used to travel back and forth by ship from England to India and sometimes the voyage would take three or even four weeks. I especially remember one voyage during the second world war when there were enemy submarines about. Those on board all knew that there might come the terrifying cry of 'submarines!' Whenever we went on that ship we all had to carry our lifejackets at all times.

On a long voyage, a ship's company becomes and inhabits a little world of its own. Small groups, cliques and coteries form in the usual way and there are nice people and those who are not so nice. People naturally make distinctions between one another. We made friends with some while inevitably there were others we did not want to know. But we all knew that if the cry 'Submarines!', went up then all of that superficial social grouping would instantly disappear. Only one central issue would remain: Life or death. In that we were all together, literally in the same boat, whatever we thought of one another. And in life itself it is the same, we are all in this together in the same situation.

That illustration, of life together aboard ship in those circumstances, is a way of expressing what the cross means. Because what happened on Good Friday was this: when Almighty God personally met us, the human race face to face,

65

it was, for practical purposes, the unanimous decision of that representative company of the human race that he must be destroyed.

The crucifixion of Jesus was not the deed of a few bad people. It was, on the contrary, the work of those who were, and are, accounted the 'best' people: the righteous, the priests, scribes, governing officials and, of course, the crowd in the streets. So unless we take the view that we are a very special case, we must consequently conclude that essentially what happened was that the human race came face to face with its Creator and its response was to seek to destroy him.

That utterly crucial and central moment in universal history is the ground on which we are compelled to say that all of us, the good and bad together, are sinners. If that was the last word, then there could be no future for the human race. The only authentic response to what happened would be what Judas did when he went out and hanged himself. What future is there for humanity if that is what we are? But, of course, it is not the last word, because the crucifixion of Jesus, while on the one hand was the act of sinful men and women, on the other hand it was the work of Christ himself who went deliberately to that meeting point to give himself up for the life of the world.

It is at that point where we are judged and condemned without distinction. The cross cannot be used as a banner for one part of humanity against another. It is the place where we are all, without distinction, unmasked as the enemies of

God. But it is also the place where to all, without distinction, there is offered the unlimited kindness and love of God.

While in a sense the first reaction to the cross is that it is a death sentence upon all of us, it is nevertheless at the same time the gift of life. So that Paul says, 'I have been crucified with Christ and I no longer live, but Christ lives in me' (Galatians 2:20). This life that I now have is not an extension, a kind of period of prolongation, given to that old self that put Jesus on the cross. It is on the contrary the gift of a new life because he who is the Creator of all life has died in order that I might live. Therefore, Paul has this to say: 'I am crucified with Christ, I am finished. I belong to a world which has no further entitlement to exist, and yet I live. But I live not because *I* live but because he died that I might live, so that the life that I now live is not mine but his, or rather it is a life that I live by faith in the Son of God who loved me and gave himself for me.'

We can only know that we are sinners because we have been forgiven. That seems to me to be absolutely fundamental. We teach the doctrine of original sin because we have been forgiven. Apart from that, the doctrine would simply be unbelievable and impossible, because it is sin itself which blinds us to sin. It is only the forgiven who can truly repent because sin blinds our eyes to the reality of who we are.

So the first and fundamental thing to be said is that we must speak of sin as something that affects and involves all humanity. This is not because we are in a position to pass judgment on anybody else, or because we have looked around the world and seen for ourselves that people are sinners. Of course, we can do that but the sinners always turn out to be other people. Rather, it is because of what happened on Calvary all those years ago that we can, and must, acknowledge that in the presence of God we have no standing except as forgiven sinners. I think that it is utterly essential to state that first, otherwise all other attempts to talk about sin puts us in the position of being judges of others.

The most systematic account of the matter is the long section in St Paul's letter to the Romans at Romans 1–7. It is after that wonderful sentence which begins, 'I am not ashamed of the gospel, because it is the power of God for the salvation of everyone who believes' (Romans 1:16) that Paul invites his readers to take a look at the world. No doubt with their full agreement, he paints a picture of that pagan world where all around there was depravity, licentiousness, fighting, quarrelling, warring factions and endemic corruption.

No doubt there would be many, especially among his Jewish readers, who would wholeheartedly agree. But he later turns upon his Jewish readers and declares in words to this effect: 'You who judge others, what about you?' (Romans 2:1) And relentlessly he convicts them of the same types of sin and finally sums up that whole section, beginning with the first part of Chapter 3, with a series of quotations from the Psalms which ultimately affirm, 'There is no-one righteous, not even one' (Romans 3:10). We all bear the same condemnation.

When he set out to examine what was at the root of that

awful situation, he did not, as so many pagan thinkers did, identify the essence of sin in such things as sexual immorality, sensuality, pride or dissenting factions. No, all of the things he describes are the fruit of a root that is fundamentally unbelief. We have become corrupt because collectively we turned our backs on the Creator and failed to trust him, instead putting our trust in things that were made. And that is a faithful rendering of the story as we have it in Genesis 3.

The essence of the story of the Fall, as it is told in that chapter, is that God called upon his created family of Adam and Eve to live simply in love and obedience and to trust him to do what was good for them. When he forbade them the fruit of that tree, the knowledge of good and evil, the essence of the temptation to which they fell was contained in the words, ' . . . you will be like God, knowing good and evil' (Genesis 3:5). In other words, do not just take it on trust but find out for yourself and make sure that you yourself know what is right or wrong. Do not take it on trust from anybody else.

That, says our Bible, is the root from which all the terrible harvest of sin ultimately comes. It is the breaking of the relationship of love, obedience and trust for which we were created, and the attempt to be our own masters and judges and to have a righteousness of our own. This is why Paul identifies the heart of the gospel as being the gift of a righteousness from God – a righteousness that is not my possession, but God's gift. That is the heart of what Paul has to say about the root, the origin, of human sin and this

69

explains what he would later say about the righteousness of God.

Then in Romans 5–6 Paul goes on to speak about our solidarity in sin. As in Adam all died, so in Christ shall all be made alive. In Adam we all sin. That statement, of our solidarity in sin, has been grievously misunderstood. This is partly because of some words of St Augustine. There are two points to notice here. First of all, in that crucial verse which says that death passed from Adam to all people, in that all sinned (Romans 5:12), the Greek words for 'in that' can, and have been, easily misunderstood or misprinted as 'in whom' – as though the sin of Adam automatically made us all guilty, which is a meaningless concept.

The true text, and all later theologians agree on this, means that it is *because, in that* we have all sinned that we are in solidarity with Adam. Secondly, Augustine disastrously connected this with Psalm 51:5 (KJV): 'and in sin did my mother conceive me.' When read in the context of the psalm this is simply a vivid way of saying, 'I am a sinner from the very beginning.' It does not mean that sin is transmitted through the act of sexual intercourse, but Augustine came close to saying something like it. And this is another misunderstanding that has distorted Western thinking on the doctrine of original sin.

What St Paul was saying, and what we surely have to recognise as truth, is that apart from conscious, individual sins resulting from our deliberate choice, we are all together, as human beings, involved in a sinful network of relationships in which we become victims of sin from the very beginning. This doctrine of original sin is something many people find abhorrent and distasteful and regard as a form of treason or breach of faith against humanity.

But any parent coping with a small child having tantrums because he or she cannot get want they want understands very well what is meant by original sin! We are all together in this network of sinful relationships which existed before we were born, and into which we are born. We are incorporated within it in the way we are brought up. We are all in this together. It is the human condition.

What is the answer to this? The answer is a righteousness from God by faith, as expressed in that fundamental verse (Romans 5:17). To put it another way, it is the gift of a relationship. It is not the gift, as it were, of a new being to ourselves as individuals. It is the gift of a new relationship to replace the one that we have broken. And here, I think, it is so tremendously important to repeat again that all our thinking has been very much shaped by the Greek conception of substance. This is the idea that behind everything that we know, or think we know, there is a kind of underlying substance which is the thing itself, and that everything, including all people and human nature, is to be understood in terms of that which is its essential substance.

But the truth, as it is in the Bible, is otherwise. The truth to be found within the Bible is that what we are constituted by are relationships. We are human beings by virtue of the fact that we are related, that we are children of God. We are

71

all the brothers and sisters, the parents and children, of one another. Human nature does not exist except in a pattern of relationships. These relationships are intrinsic to humankind.

To make clear what I mean, consider this illustration from physics. We all know that for centuries scientists and thinkers had sought to identify the atom as the essential unit of matter, beyond which it was not possible to go. The atom was the ultimate substance underlying all matter. We now know that the atom is not just the smallest particle of a chemical element but part of a network of dynamic relationships between particles which are not themselves matter, but electrical charges. So even matter itself ultimately consists of a pattern of intricate relationships. At the other end of the cosmic scale when we use the word 'God' we are not, properly speaking, referring to some kind of divine substance. We are instead more truthfully and accurately referring to a pattern of relationships between Father, Son and Holy Spirit in complete and absolute love and communion. This is the proper designation of the word 'God'.

From this point of view we can see that the Fall is essentially the attempt by human beings, whose only reality lies in their relationship of dependence upon God, to establish a reality for themselves. This, so to speak, enables them to stand on their own feet in relation to God and to make up their own minds on good and evil and not simply exist in a relationship of love and obedience to the Creator.

That is why the answer to the appalling fact of sin is precisely the establishment of a new relationship: a righteousness from God by faith. This does not involve a righteousness which is mine so that I can say I am a righteous person, but is of a different kind of righteousness. It is a righteousness that comprises the fact that God has accepted us in Jesus Christ and that in faith we believe and accept. It is that relationship between holy God and sinful us which constitutes the only righteousness that there can ever be.

How has this been brought about? First of all we need to look at the Old Testament background to the story told in the Gospels. The Old Testament is full of terrible accounts of the wickedness of human beings, from the first family where one brother murders the other to all those evil acts that finally caused God to try to wipe out the whole world in a flood, preserving only a righteous remnant. Again he destroyed the Tower of Babel when the human family attempted to establish its own authority with a tower that reached up to heaven.

In a sense the whole theme of the Old Testament can be described as God's response – the 'passion of God'. It is the passion of a holy God over his sinful family. It begins with that terrible cry in the Garden of Eden on that first evening when God called out for Adam, 'Where are you?' (Genesis 3:9) It is the agonised cry of a parent whose child has gone astray and is lost.

Throughout the Old Testament there is this passion of God calling upon a family to leave its home, to leave the things that are seen and relied upon and to learn to live a new life simply by faith. That family had been safeguarded

73

and rescued out of slavery in Egypt and brought into a good and pleasant land, but that family defiled this land with their sin and rebelled time and again against their loving Creator. God, in his agony, sometimes threatened them with dreadful punishments, sometimes putting his family under terrible disciplines and then again repenting and wooing its members like a lover pursuing his bride. This is seen in that marvellous passage in Hosea: 'How can I give you up, Ephraim . . . all my compassion is aroused' (Hosea 11:8).

Then you have those marvellous passages in the latter part of Isaiah, the so-called servant songs, which picture the servant of the Lord – which should have been Israel if it had been true to its calling – as bearing all the sin of the world in that servant's own heart. Finally, we come to our Lord himself in whom all these prophecies signalling the passion of God are made flesh and blood in the life of this human being, Jesus Christ. We see him calling Israel to fulfil the purpose for which it was called – to be God's servant people for all the nations. When that calling was denied, Jesus went alone to his cross to bear in his own body and soul the passion of God for this sinful world.

So the one who is Lord of all was humiliated, cursed, cast out and executed as a criminal and blasphemer. And in his agony and desolation he cried out, 'My God, my God, why have you forsaken me' (Matthew 27:46). Entering right into the God-forsaken state of this sinful family of God, descending into the very depths so that nothing of God's creation might be left unredeemed, God raised him from the dead to a new life and exalted him to heaven as Lord. He sent forth the Holy Spirit on the day of Pentecost to fill the church with the knowledge that this crucified man, rejected by the world, was the mighty God and the Lord of all. And so the church sets forth on its mission to proclaim the mystery of salvation.

What I am trying to explain is that what happened is a fact. God's victory is to be considered an actuality before we begin to advance our theories on how to explain it. It is a fact of history that these things occurred. In the outpouring of the Holy Spirit after the ascension of Jesus, the church was given the assurance and authority to preach to the world that the power of sin had been broken. The righteousness of God had been given to us so that we, the unholy, might live in the love and fellowship of the holy God.

I am absolutely sure that when we speak of the atonement wrought in Jesus Christ we are talking of things that go beyond human language, because language is simply not up to the job of explaining or articulating something which is ultimately the contradiction of all reason, and that is the concept of sin. If we could, as it were, incorporate sin into a coherent rational structure of thought, it would no longer be sin. We are dealing with an ultimate, a surd, something which simply cannot be apprehended by linguistic or even mathematical structures and fitted into any rational scheme. All our attempts to comprehend what was done through the atonement, in terms of fully thought out conceptual patterns, must therefore fall short of the truth. These attempts, however, can point us towards the truth.

One of the great metaphors of reconciliation used in the Scriptures is the notion of ransom which often depicts the redeeming of a slave from his or her master through the generosity of another. It is an image used by our Lord himself. This metaphor was charged with enormous emotional weight in a society where slavery was so common. But if you try to push this metaphor to its logical conclusion, the question arises, 'To whom was the ransom paid?' Some early theologians suggested it was paid to God while others insisted it went to the devil. But neither can be accepted because to argue that it was a ransom paid to God implies that God had to be placated in order to forgive us. And that would assume that there was antagonism between the Son and the Father, which is wholly contrary to the Christian faith. To argue that it was paid to the devil overstates Satan's authority.

Another metaphor is that of substitution – of another who has died in our place. This again embraces a deep and intrinsic element of truth. And yet it cannot finally explain what happened. It is so clear in the teachings of our Lord himself that while he goes before us, and it is he alone who can meet the ultimate enemy in that final battle, we are not excused from that encounter. It is precisely the opposite – that we may be enabled to follow him, to take up the cross and go the way that he has gone.

There is next the metaphor of sacrifice. This is fully developed in the letter to the Hebrews which so clearly fulfils the Old Testament regulations with regard to sacrifice. We see Jesus as the ultimate sacrifice to the Father. But, once again, we must be careful not to understand or express this as if antagonism existed between the Son and the Father, as though the Father needed to be placated.

It is one of the significant little features of the Old Testament use of the word 'expiation' or 'atonement' that the Hebrew verb, constantly used in relation to God, is never used in the form which puts God as the object. It is used, for example, where Jacob wanted to placate Esau, who was on his way to meet him with an armed band, and Jacob sent a collection of gifts ahead of him. There the word was used, as he tried to placate his brother, but it was never used with God as its object. We find that it is always used in a subtle, indirect form – that God has provided a sacrifice, to make atonement concerning sin – so that there is no question of the Son, as it were, placating the Father. On the contrary, the atoning work of Christ is also the work of the Father.

Although we can never fully explain the atonement by using human language, all these different metaphors nevertheless help us get a little closer to the centre of this mystery. I have often said that one of the most helpful of them, is the one concerning the Old Testament Hebrew word for the 'mercy seat', the place where the sinner could be received by the holy God. This is translated in Romans 3 as the place of propitiation. Surely here we come near to the heart of what was done there. It has created a place where we who are sinners, and we are still sinners, can nevertheless be in fellowship with God who is holy, because in this act the Son of God, in loving obedience to the Father, has taken his place right where we are in our lost state. He has therefore made possible a *koinonia*, a communion, in the Holy Spirit, in which we share the very life of God himself, sinners though we are.

This word *koinonia* which we translate as fellowship, the fellowship of the Holy Spirit, is actually a word which means common sharing in a property. If I and three brothers jointly own a field it would be said that we had *koinonia* in that field. When we refer to the fellowship of the Holy Spirit we are speaking of a shared participation in the actual life of God the Holy Spirit. That place, of course, is the church. This is where we gather in the name of Jesus. We hear his words, and in the sacrament which he has ordained, we partake of his dying and his victorious resurrection and triumph over death. This is the place where we know and experience justification and sanctification.

Justification is being recognised by God. This is not because we are in ourselves just, or righteous, but because in this act in Jesus Christ he has accepted us as just, as righteous. It is a righteousness which is on the one hand the sheer gift of God and on the other hand is accepted in faith. It is never our possession, but something received moment by moment, by faith in what God has done for us in Jesus Christ.

It is also the place of sanctification. Again, this does not mean that sanctification is a process by which we gradually become holy in ourselves, as though we could obtain a holiness which was not simply God's gift, but was our personal characteristic. That would be a contradiction at the very heart of the gospel. It is interesting to note that when Paul puts the words for justification and sanctification together it is sanctification which comes first: 'You were washed, you were sanctified, you were justified . . .' (1 Corinthians 6:11). Both the words sanctification and justification refer to a relationship with God, not to something that we possess within ourselves. The holiness which is the proper mark of a disciple of Jesus is not, and can never be, something that we possess in that way. So we can never assert that perfect holiness, something which was so central to John Wesley's preaching in the eighteenth century is, so to speak, a designation, a kind of personal possession. That perfect holiness is simply the relationship of faithful dependence upon the sanctifying grace of God.

It seems to me that this all adds up to a most joyful way of preaching the doctrine of original sin. G. K. Chesterton, that quick witted and provocative English critic, novelist and poet, talked about 'the good news of original sin'. What did he mean by that? Let me put it in a rather jocular way. If the whole lot of us are nothing more than a bunch of escaped convicts, which by analogy is what we are, then there is room for an enormous amount of joy, of celebration of being alive and of much merriment in the life of the church. We do not have to go around pretending to be righteous. We have no place at all except as forgiven sinners who have been embraced, accepted and loved by the holy God. And as the Psalms so often remind us, this is something which can only lead us onwards to singing and dancing.

We are delivered from the unbearable burden of trying to be ourselves, wrapped up in our own righteousness. We have one thing and one thing only to do, to believe and to give our lives in a moment by moment offering of thanks to the one who loves us and who laid down his life for us. And that is what the Christian life is. Yes, it's good news!

CHAPTER FIVE

The Church

One, Holy, Apostolic

In the previous chapter I referred to one of the ways in which St Paul spoke about what was done on the cross when he used the Greek word which translates the Old Testament Hebrew word for the 'mercy seat'. In the New Testament the word is translated as 'propitiation'. One of the most helpful ways to comprehend what Christ did for us on the cross lies in the knowledge and understanding that he has created a place where sinful men and women, despite their sins, may be accepted by God and enabled to live and rejoice in his presence. It is, if you like, the continuation of the ministry of Jesus who received sinners and ate and drank with them. The church is the place where this still happens.

The church is obviously an integral part of the gospel. Nobody becomes a Christian by first of all studying the doctrines of atonement and justification by faith, and so forth, and then at the end of the 'course' looking around for some place to make contact. On the contrary, we become Christians because in one way or another the work of the Holy Spirit has drawn us into some kind of existing Christian fellowship. The church precedes our faith, and as always, the gospel is not a set of disembodied ideas or a set of words. It is always a concrete reality in history: a reality which we call the church.

The New Testament word for the church is the Greek word *ekklesia*, which also means 'assembly', and from which words such as ecclesiastical and so forth are derived. And it is worth looking at the background of that word. The Bible of the early church was the Greek of what we call the Old Testament. In it they would have read of the congregation, the whole assembly, of the people of Israel. These Old Testament meanings were rendered in the Greek by two words – *synagogos* and *ekklesia*. They might have taken either *synagogos* or *ekklesia* because they understood themselves to be the congregation which had its origin in God's calling of Abraham. They did not see themselves as a new society. They were the congregation of the people of Israel which was enlarged to include the Gentiles, as God had promised to both the patriarchs and prophets.

They could, as I have said, chosen either of those two words. There is one place in the New Testament where the word synagogue, *synagogos*, is used, but otherwise they always used the other word *ekklesia*, which the Greek Old Testament uses. And perhaps there were two reasons for that. One might be that the word synagogue was already used by the Jews for their congregations. The other was that the word *ekklesia* was a secular word which described the assembly of all the people.

In the Greek city states the affairs of the city were settled in the assembly, as we see in the latter chapters of Acts, and that assembly was called the *ekklesia*, the calling out of the people. That is its literal meaning. In Acts the assembly was called by what we would now refer to as the town clerk and all the citizens were expected to attend. But this is the assembly called, not by the town clerk, but by God. And so the church is constantly referred to in the Greek as *ekklesia tou Theou*, the assembly of God, the assembly which God called. That was the phrase the first Christians used to describe their togetherness as the continuation of the congregation of the people of Israel.

This explains an important little point in the New Testament – that the same name is used both for an individual local church and for the church as a whole. We ourselves tend to use two words. We use the term 'congregation' when we speak of a local gathering and we are inclined to use the word 'church' for the universal body. But the early church had no such distinction. You will notice this in the Acts and in Paul's letters. He speaks of the churches of Asia, or the church of Asia. It is not that the individual churches are branches of the church. The church is that act of God gathering his people in each place, and in all places. So it is necessary to have this dynamic picture, which is the real inner meaning of this biblical language.

Everywhere God is gathering his people through Jesus Christ into this place of atonement where it is possible for sinful men and women to have fellowship with God. But that action is happening both locally and universally. And that is also why the church is never designated by any other adjectives

83

except the name of the place and the name of the one who calls it.

It is the assembly of God in Corinth, the assembly of God in Ephesus, the congregation of God in Colosse. That is how the church is defined. It is defined by the one who calls it and by where this calling takes place.

When it was proposed to call the church by any name other than the name of God and the name of the place – as, for example, in Corinth, (1 Corinthians 3) where people said we are of Peter's party, of Apollos' or Paul's party – Paul was scandalised. He effectively said, 'You are carnal. You have dismembered the body of Christ.' Paul was affronted by the thought that anyone should attach any name except that of Christ and the place.

So the church in each place is the catholic church, the universal church, and not a branch. It is the catholic church because God is here calling it. And where God is, you cannot say that it is a branch of a church; it is *the* church. This means that by its very nature, the church is one. There is one God and one Lord Jesus Christ, and there is one place of atonement, not many, and therefore the church is one. But here, of course, we come to the sad story of disunity. We know that the church throughout its history has become divided.

It is worthwhile running over the main divisions. The first great partition happened in the fourth and fifth centuries when the churches outside the Roman Empire, which could not take part in the theological discussions that defined the nature of Christ, became separated. I am thinking, for example, of the Armenians, Assyrians, Syrians, Copts and Ethiopians, many of whom would probably never have become separated but for that tremendous political divide.

You can well understand that when the Roman and Persian empires were either at war or in a state of political hostility, Christians in Persia, Armenia or India might well have been suspected of being stooges of the ruling empire. If you lived in the Roman Empire these people were regarded as foreigners. So although there were doctrinal differences, this was principally a political-motivated division, which has left us with what we call the 'lesser eastern churches'.

The second great division came in the eleventh century with the mutual excommunications of Byzantium and Rome. The two halves of the Empire had been drifting apart for a long time, but it is important to remember that from the point of view of the eastern churches the Roman Catholic Church was, for two reasons, a schismatic body.

First the Roman church made an addition to the Nicene creed without consulting the whole body of the church. They added the so-called 'Filioque clause': the words, 'and from the Son'. This related to whether the Holy Spirit proceeds from the Father (which both churches agreed upon) *as well as* the Son. This still remains a deeply resented schismatic act in the minds of eastern Christians. The second reason was the action of Pope Leo III in crowning Charlamagne in St Peter's Church on Christmas Day in AD 800 as emperor when there was already an emperor on the throne in Constantinople. These two theological and political acts were seen as schismatic. To this day in the Eastern part of Christendom – in the Russian, Greek, Serbian and other major orthodox churches – there remains a deep sense of resentment against the Church of Rome. In some ways this division goes much deeper than that within the Western church – between the Roman Catholics and the churches of the Reformation.

In the sixteenth century the third division occurred, with which we are all so familiar: the Reformation which separated Northern and Southern Europe from each other. And then in the nineteenth century, especially in the United States, the idea of a denomination developed, as though Christians could quite contentedly live in separate bodies, regarding themselves all as different branches of the same church. That was the fourth major point of schism to further divide the church.

How are we to understand the issues that divided the church? I suppose it is helpful to draw attention to three great emphases that are not mutually contradictory – which are all properly part of the reality of the church – but have become separated and put against one another. I am speaking of what one might roughly call the Catholic, the Protestant and the Pentecostal emphases.

Look first at the Catholic emphasis. Jesus said to his disciples, 'You did not choose me, but I chose you . . .' (John 15:16). The church is not a body of people who have decided that they are going to follow Jesus. The church is that body created by Jesus. He called them apostles, consecrating them and sending them out into the world to make disciples of all nations. It was a specific and particular body historically created, formed and sent forth by Jesus Christ. He gave them the sacraments of baptism and the Lord's Supper, and they went out and preached. Subsequently they appointed their successors from those among the believers they found to be fit for that office.

The emphasis here is that the church exists not as a body which we have created or constituted. It is there as the body which Jesus Christ himself sent into the world. But some people set themselves up and say, 'We will have our own leadership. We have consecrated our own bishops and we will do our own thing.' Is that the church? Surely the church is something that is given, with its objective reality, which we must clearly embrace if we are to find salvation. That is the Catholic emphasis.

One of the most vivid expressions of this emphasis is to be found in the autobiography of John Henry Newman, the great Anglican leader, who in 1845 became a Roman Catholic and led many others to follow him. If you read the autobiography of this writer, poet and historian you will see that this man was passionately concerned with the overriding question: 'Which is the true church?' He reasoned that if one was not part of the true church then one was not saved. As a result of his agonised and reasoned arguments he concluded that the Roman Catholic Church was the true church and that all the others, however excellent, were not the authentic church. So the church is defined, at least in part, by its valid historical succession. It can show that it is the same body

DISCOVERING TRUTH IN A CHANGING WORLD

which Jesus sent out into the world, not something that has been shaped by any kind of innovation.

Against this you have the tremendous issues that arose so strongly at the time of the Reformation: that the church may well have a valid apostolic succession, but it could lose its way. Its bishops may have been consecrated by bishops who in turn were consecrated by bishops, and so on, until you reach those who were consecrated by the original apostles, and yet it still might fall into error and sin. Episcopal consecration could not guarantee the reality of the church. In the robust language that people used at the time of the Reformation, the Scots reformer John Knox (1505–72) declared, 'Lineal descent is no mark by which the true church may be distinguished from the kirk malignant, that horrible harlot!' Well, theological discussions were conducted in a lively manner in those days, but that was the essential emphasis.

The point the Reformers made was that the church was something created by the action of the living Christ. Its existence did not simply depend upon historic succession but was created by the living power of the gospel, mediated through the word and the sacraments of the gospel. This dynamic conception of the church had enormous power. It brought about a tremendous renewal, but also, of course, a tremendous division in the life of the church. The danger is that it seems to neglect that which the Catholic emphasis affirms. It is in danger of making the church something which, as it were, happens moment by moment, or fails to happen, but not something which is a given historical reality continuing through history.

Next there is what I call the Pentecostal emphasis. You may have correct apostolic succession and correct doctrine as well as properly administered sacraments, and yet the living power of the Spirit may be absent. Are you then the true church? There is a grim little story in the Acts of a man who was claiming to cast out evil spirits in the name of Jesus and Paul, and several demoniacs attacked him, exclaiming, 'Jesus I know and I know about Paul, but who are you?' (Acts 19:15) Do you have the authentic presence of the living Spirit or not?

Each of those three emphases is valid. They have their authentication in the gospel. Yet each, taken alone, can lead to a vital loss of substance. The Catholic emphasis, by itself, can produce something which has no life in it, which is formal and dead. The Protestant emphasis can produce something very lively but which has no sense of unity. It can break apart, especially when the whole thing depends upon correct doctrine. The history of the Protestant church is one of continual division over the detail of doctrine so that the unity of the church disappears from view.

In the Pentecostal tradition the danger is that one emphasises experience, individual personal experience, without paying sufficient attention to these questions: 'What is it we are experiencing? What is the reality with which we are dealing?' In our kind of society, especially with its tendency to subjectivism and relativism, there is a real danger that this emphasis, taken by itself, can lead into the church dissolving into 'what I feel'.

With great respect to our good friends in the Methodist church I think one has to recognise that this dissolving has sometimes happened. John Wesley's great revival saw a tremendous outpouring of the power of the Spirit, manifested in the transformation of lives and in the manifold gifts of the Spirit. But Christianity has often dissolved into something defined as 'what I feel good about' – merely a kind of personal subjective experience. This is because at times insufficient attention has been given both to doctrine – to what we believe, the truth to which we have committed ourselves – and to the given continuity and reality of the universal church. These three elements, integral to the fullness of the gospel, can nevertheless lead us to division and mutual suspicion when they are separated. The result is that we profoundly suspect one another of not being true to the reality of the church.

How can we overcome these divisions? We cannot escape the force of the words our Lord used on the night of his passion, ' . . . that all of them may be one, Father, just as you are in me and I am in you. May they also be in us so that the world may believe . . .' (John 17:21). We cannot deny that it is the intention of our Lord that the church should be in such ways a visible unity, that the world may recognise that this is the place of atonement where sin is forgiven and where we can be reconciled to one another. This is the place of which Jesus spoke: 'I, when I am lifted up from the earth, will draw all people to myself' (John 12:32). We cannot escape the vital importance of unity, no matter how much we may be disappointed in the face of difficulty.

But let us not forget that we are now living in the first age of Christian reunion. The entire history of the church over the past centuries has been one long story of continual division. We are the privileged ones who live in an age where for the first time people are beginning to come together, though perhaps slowly and hesitantly, and to recognise one another in Christ despite their many differences.

How does God enable us to restore the unity of the church? The problem is that each of us is bound to confess that a church to which he or she belongs is the church of God. This is because that specific church was the one that drew that particular person to Christ. I cannot deny that. And the temptation for us is that we look at one another and perhaps say, 'In this respect you lack something. You lack one of the essential marks of the church.' It might be in regard to doctrine or apostolic succession or in relation to the place of the Spirit in the life of one's church, but we tend to say to each other, 'If you can correct yourself at this point, then we can unite.'

But there is an important difference between asserting that something is a proper mark of the church and maintaining that something is essential to the church. Something can be a proper mark of the church – and these three things I have mentioned are proper marks of the church, they properly belong to the nature of the church – but if you say they are essential, then you are suggesting that without them there is no church. And none of us has been willing to draw the logical conclusion of that.

From the Roman Catholic point of view, in the report of the Anglican Roman Catholic International Commission it is said, for example, that recognition of the Papacy or recognition of a certain doctrine of the Eucharist is 'essential' as a pre-requisite of union. You are really saying that without these there is no church. 'Essential' means exactly that, fundamental or absolutely necessary. The logic of this kind of thinking would be to conclude that those churches which lack these things ought to have disappeared – as a branch cut from the vine perishes – and if a church lacks something essential to its life then it ought not to exist. And all our excommunications of one another, such as the excommunications exchanged between the patriarch of Constantinople and the Pope of Rome in 1054, if God had 'validated' them, would have meant that these churches would have disappeared and thus no longer existed as part of the church. But they have not disappeared.

Surely we must accept the fact that the church exists only by the mercy of God, only by his grace to sinners and not by its fulfilment of any of the conditions for the fullness of the church. It is, as I have suggested, the basic picture of the place of atonement: where God receives sinners into his fellowship. Does that not mean, therefore, that the way for us to restore the unity of the church is that we accept one another as God seems to have accepted us? Let us accordingly accept one another as we are, acknowledging the many ways in which we fall short of God's purpose for the church and then, having accepted one another as we are, seek to correct, reform and build up one another in the faith.

There is a kind of relaxed and tolerant easy-going way, which I fear is becoming all too popular, which finds expression when we simply say, 'Yes, let us all accept one another, because God has accepted us.' And we leave it at that. It is the equivalent of our saying, 'Shall we go on sinning, so that grace may increase? (Romans 6:1) If God has given grace to churches which are sinful, which lack something that belongs properly to the church, let us just carry on and God will continue to give us his grace. This notion is unthinkable: 'Shall we continue in sin, that grace may abound?' St Paul's reply is vehement, 'God forbid' (v.2). It is unthinkable. The mercy of God towards churches which lack that which belongs properly to the church, should not lead us to contentment. Rather it should lead us to repentance and to a willingness not merely to accept one another, but to correct one another. We should therefore hold one another up to the reality of the gospel itself so that God may make of us what he intends us to be.

Looking at the present situation, some general points can be made about the church in Europe. If we look at the church in parts of the world such as Africa, Asia and the Pacific Islands where it continues to grow rapidly, the situation is different. But in considering the situation in Europe I think we have to agree that the Roman Catholic Church, with a kind of stubborn intransigence, is still a tremendous power but is nevertheless facing severe internal contradictions and crises.

I think undoubtedly the mainline Protestant churches in Europe are in decline and that the main growing parts of the church in Europe are the evangelical and charismatic bodies, both within the churches and in the various 'parachurch' organisations, fellowships and associations, which are springing up so luxuriantly around us.

At this point it is important to say one word about the importance of the Catholic tradition. When I was a student it was the Anglo-Catholic wing of the Church of England which was strong and vigorous, producing the best scholars, many of the best priests and generally setting the pace. Evangelicals were a relatively small and rather frightened minority. The position today is almost exactly the opposite.

The evangelical wing of the church is strong, growing and confident, and the Catholic wing of the church, especially following the crisis over the admission of women to the priesthood, is on the defensive. And I think that exactly at this point, we recognise the importance of the Catholic tradition, the objective reality of the church and its sacraments as something which is given, and not just a matter of my personal experience.

I have often been a bit turned off when some of my friends have spoken of a Eucharistic service as if the important thing about it was whether or not it had personal meaning, as though essentially it was a kind of subjective experience. If you compare that with what St Paul says in 1 Corinthians about participation in the Eucharist, where he says that if you take part in it without discerning the body, it is not merely that nothing happens, it is that you are under judgment. Whatever happens when you take part in the Eucharist it is not that nothing happens, something happens! (1 Corinthians 11:27–29)

Either you are built up in your life in Christ, or you are judged, but an objective reality exists there. I think it is important that we recover our sense of this in the face of the subjectivism and relativism of so much of our culture. I say this because currently it is the evangelical and charismatic parts of the church which are, thank God, so strong and confident and bearing so much fruit.

I think we are all uncertain about how to proceed in the matter of Christian unity. This is because the movements towards organic unity, so promising around fifty years ago, seem in large measure to have petered out. We have to discover new ways and means to express our unity across the board, from the Roman Catholic and Orthodox churches, to the evangelical and charismatic churches where so much of the main growth is now going on. Perhaps at first these new ways can be very informal. But undoubtedly we are faced with one of the greatest challenges of the present time.

The real issue that divides Christians in the United Kingdom today is not between Catholics and evangelicals or Protestants and charismatics, but the difference between those who believe that there is a gospel and those who have ceased to believe that. On the one hand there are those who believe unequivocally in a God-given reality: 'For God so loved the world, that he gave his one and only Son' (John 3:16), and that here is the place of atonement. I think that Catholics, evangelicals and charismatics have that in common. On the other hand, there are sadly a great many Christians in the United Kingdom who have lost the sense of there being a real God, and have allowed their faith to dissolve away into opinions and subjective experiences, with no real gospel.

Let me finish with five affirmations that sum up what I want to say. The first is the one with which I began: the historic reality of the Christian church. It is important to stress this point because when you listen to the radio, watch television or read the newspapers, you soon realise the church is often regarded as a fairly marginal phenomenon interested only in gaining popularity. The inevitable, and almost only, question the media asks is whether or not certain activities are going to make churches more popular. It is as though they are looked upon as a passing phenomenon and if they are not popular enough they will disappear. How absurd, especially when you remember that the church has outlived mighty empires, infamous totalitarian structures and great philosophical systems. Within twenty years the things that today seem to occupy the whole horizon of public thinking become half-remembered phantoms, mere ephemera, of a past age. But the church will still be there.

The church is an historic reality, beginning with God's call to Abraham and continuing through the ministry of prophets and apostles right down the ages until now. And whether or not the church is popular, big or small, is relatively unimportant. The fact of this great rock, this anvil upon which so many hammers have been worn out, this given reality, needs to be at the centre of our thinking as Christians.

Secondly, the church is a body of sinful men and women. It is a body of sinners whom God calls saints. St Paul usually starts his letters by saying something like this: 'Paul, called to be an apostle to the church in Corinth, called to be saints.' The Greek actually says, 'Called apostle, called saints.' It is not in the Greek, 'Called to *be* saints' it is 'called saints' – *klatos apostolos, kletois hagiois.* In other words, God calls them saints.

They may not look like it but God calls them saints and it is what God calls them that matters. They are sinners! Yes we are! But God calls us saints because God has made us his own – that is the whole meaning of atonement. Of course, the church is always going to be a bunch of sinners. It has never been anything else. And it is very easy to become completely pessimistic about the church. We have to be realistic and not pretend that the church is anything other than it is. But we also have to be faithful, knowing that it is what God says that goes. If God has called us saints, made us his own, given us his gift of atonement in Jesus Christ, then that defines who and what we are.

Above all, let us not escape with this idea of an invisible church. The invisible church is an attractive idea because the visible church is the people God has chosen, and as we know, he has chosen some pretty funny characters. The invisible church has the great advantage that 'I' choose who belongs to it. It is the church of the people that I think are the real Christians and that, of course, is very comforting, but that is not the church. The church is that body of sinners, whom God has called and chosen to be saints, to belong to him.

Thirdly, the church is defined by its centre, not by its boundaries. When you begin to define the church by its boundaries, you get into all kinds of legalistic difficulties: 'Was that person baptised? Was the one who baptised that person ordained by a bishop? Was that bishop consecrated in the apostolic succession? Was the right statement of faith signed? Did the person concerned have the right kind of spiritual experience?' These are all relevant questions but the ultimate questions are: 'Is he or she absolutely committed to Christ? Is Christ absolutely fundamental for him or her?' By that I mean Christ as he is known to us in the Scriptures, not a Christ that we imagine.

I am afraid there are many people who talk about Christ, but not about the Christ we meet in the Gospels. They talk of an ideal figure they have manufactured for themselves. I am talking about the Christ who is known to us in the Gospels. We know what he said and did and we know what he calls us to do.

Essentially I believe the church is constituted by its relationship to Jesus Christ. If a person tells me that for him or her, Jesus is final and decisive, then I must regard that person as a brother or sister in Christ. From that point, I can begin to ask, 'Then how do you reconcile what you do with Jesus? How can you reconcile what you say with Jesus?' There is a basis on which we can correct one another and build one another up, but it is the centre that defines the whole thing.

The fourth point is that the church is a sign and an instrument – a foretaste of the kingdom of God. The church is not itself the kingdom of God, nor is the kingdom something completely separate from the church. When we separate the kingdom of God from the church, then the church becomes some kind of ideology, a sort of programme or a social or political utopia. The church is both the sign and the instrument, and therefore the foretaste. It is a sign, and a sign always points away from itself. If you are in Manchester you will not see a sign pointing to Manchester. It is when you are elsewhere that you have a sign. So the church is a sign in that it points to something which is not itself but is a foretaste of the reality of God's reign. It is a guiding light or it may be an instrument in the hands of God for doing his will in the world, an instrument of the kingdom. It is both of those because it is a foretaste. The church is that fellowship within which we enjoy a foretaste of the freedom, the joy, the holiness of God's kingdom. And because it is a taste or experience of something to be enjoyed in advance, it can be looked upon as both a sign and an instrument.

My fifth and final point is that the church – and this is the proper sense of the invisible church – is in communion with the saints who have gone before. This is an element that we are in danger of losing in the reformed Protestant churches. We must not lose this most precious thing, that the churches remain in communion with those who have gone before us on the way of faith, who wait with us for the final victory of Christ, for the resurrection of the body and the coming of the new heavens and new earth.

It ought to be a living part of our life in Christ, that we share in the communion of the saints, in the fellowship of those who have gone before us and who inspire us as they, and we, look to Jesus and to his final victory, of which we have the foretaste, right now, in the gift of the Holy Spirit.

CHAPTER SIX

The Last Things

The Kingdom of God

The Bible is a story. It is the story of all things, from the beginning to the end. It is a faithful account of the Creation, the making of all things. It is also a narrative of the Fall, which alienated our world from its Creator. It is a recital of God's redeeming work and of that consummation he has promised.

We are now approaching a discussion of the 'last things' – death, resurrection, immortality, the end of the world and final judgment – what is technically called eschatology. This term is derived from the Greek word *eschatos* which means the end. Theologians love to throw around words like eschatology, perhaps to remind us of their scholarship and erudition. So just in case you might want to sound a little more learned in your next conversation, I offer this one quite freely – for what it's worth!

There is nothing more significant and decisive for moulding and defining our way of understanding than the story that we tell of ourselves. It is pivotal. Europe has been defined and characterised by its own story which has made it distinct from Asia. But, of course, the account that Europeans have given of themselves over these past two hundred years has not been the story of the Bible, but rather of what we have chosen to call 'progress'. This doctrine of 'progress', which has its origins in the eighteenth century, has shaped our thinking from the middle of the eighteen century until the First World War. To a large extent, we are still immersed in it. We find it difficult to view this cult of progress with detachment and often fail to shake our minds out of it and to recognise that it is a very recent story. It is a story culturally unknown in many parts of the world, and it is certainly not the story the Bible tells.

It is this reverence of 'progress' which causes us to think automatically that the things and events of earlier times are crude, primitive and less developed. We habitually and mechanically believe that the things of the present and future are, and always will be, more refined and better developed. We unconsciously think that everything old fashioned and out of date is by definition inferior. This whole mode of thinking is expressed in words like progress, development, evolution, growth and so forth. We have been conditioned into thinking of our story in those terms, as a continuous upward movement. C.S. Lewis aptly termed this phenomenon 'chronological snobbery' – that anything modern or recent is always better than something ancient.

At the same time, there is another, older story which still persists in the back of our minds. This is about how things were somehow much better in the past. It is a story told especially by old people, but a very familiar story. This is also an ancient story which suggests the idea of a golden age in the past. Human history is felt to be a journey of descent from that golden age to the present.

In society today much depends upon the relative importance between the old and the young. In most traditional societies the old are supposed to be wise and their point of view is respected. But with the rise of the doctrine of progress in the eighteenth century, as a direct result of the Enlightenment and the Age of Reason, a conscious movement arose throughout Europe to take the education of the young out of the hands of parents and churches. A system of government-controlled state education was developed that inculcated into successive generations a different view of the world. The whole idea that education should be the responsibility of the government is a very recent concept and is one of the implications of that new doctrine of progress.

Behind both these stories there is a still more ancient one, perhaps the most popular, which combines the idea of progress with that of a golden age in the past. And that is to see life and nature as a circle, a continuous and inexorable wheel, where things rise, develop, mature, decay and finally fall. It is, of course, a natural way of understanding ourselves because it is what we always see in the natural world around us. Plants and animals, everything in the natural world, is seen to go through a changing cycle. There is a time for renewal and growth, then of maturity leading to decay. But then another cycle begins, so that we have the feeling that we are moving, but in fact we are going nowhere because ultimately we are part of this great turning wheel of nature.

The most rigorous development of this worldview is found in Indian thought with the fundamental concept of reincarnation. None of the great religious movements – Buddhism, Sikhism, the modern religious movements in India – has questioned the idea of reincarnation. The different schools of thought in Hinduism represent different proposals for escaping from this endless, meaningless cycle of birth and rebirth. Escaping from this appalling and terrible prospect – of ceaseless birth and rebirth, where in each incarnation we are compelled to suffer the consequences of the deeds of our previous life – forms the background of all Indian religion.

One of the extraordinary ironies of today is that significant numbers of people in the Western world are trying to revive belief in the idea of reincarnation. They would thus imprison themselves on that eternal wheel from which Indian religion has spent all its energies in trying to escape. It is one of the stark illustrations of the fact that if the story of the Bible no longer guides and directs us, we shall return inevitably to Asia and become, again, simply the western end of Asia.

But, of course, the story we have told over the past two hundred years, the way of understanding our history as a chronicle of progress and development, has this one fatal flaw: we shall not be around at the end. However much we might think of history in terms of a glorious future for the human race, one thing is quite certain – we shall not be there. This has inevitably resulted in the separation of our vision of the future of society from that of our personal future.

That is the root of the privatisation of religion about which we often complain. If for the sake of argument the real meaning of history were to be realised in the year 20,000, when we shall not be alive, then we have to ask about the goal of personal history, and that then becomes a separate issue. It becomes the idea of a personal survival of death, because one has dropped out of the history of the world. So we have this dividing of these two eschatologies – the public and the private – and there seems to be no way of bringing them together because inevitably one has dropped out of the story of the world before it has been completed.

What is unique about the eschatology of the Bible – the vision of the end which we have in Revelation, the last book of the Bible – is that it draws together and unites the public and private. It is the holy city into which the kings of the earth bring their glory. It is therefore the consummation of the whole history of civilisation, because the literal meaning of the one civilisation is the making of a city. It is all these things, but it is also the consummation of every personal life. It is the place where the tears will be wiped from each and every eye and where we shall be with God and see him face to face.

How is it that the Bible is able to bring together that which we have split asunder in our telling of the story? The answer is that since it was sin and death that created the split, it is sin and death that separates us from the human story before it reaches its end. It is only because the Bible tells the story of how sin and death have been conquered that it can give us an eschatology which includes both the public and private.

105

To put it very crudely and bluntly – and we will develop this in Revelation – we see that the end does not come as the result of a smooth and upward progress, but only after judgment and catastrophe: the fire of judgment that burns everything. In other words, only after the cross comes the resurrection.

Consider the biblical understanding of the end. Take a look at it as a whole. If we examine the Old Testament we know that its great central theme is that the Lord reigns. The Lord who delivered us out of slavery in Egypt is the Lord of heaven and earth and in the end all nations and all peoples will acknowledge him. But overwhelmingly, the Old Testament sees the end as something which is in this world. It is a picture of a renewed world. 'Every valley shall be raised up, every mountain and hill made low' (Isaiah 40:4); 'The wolf will live with the lamb, the leopard will lie down with the goat . . . and a little child will lead them' (Isaiah 11:6); 'Everyone will sit under their own vine and under their own fig tree, and no-one will make them afraid' (Micah 4:4). All these pictures in the Old Testament of the promised end, are pictures in this world. It is true that there are hints of something beyond death, not strongly developed but nevertheless present.

The events of the Maccabean wars seems to have made the decisive difference. In the struggle to overcome the appalling tyranny of the pagan rule of the Greek emperors, thousands of loyal Jews were slain because they faithfully and courageously refused to break the Sabbath by fighting on that day. It became impossible to believe that all these unfortunate people who perished in faith should be excluded from the consummation for which they had fought and died. It is therefore in this intertestamental period that the doctrine of the resurrection of the dead came to occupy a key place in Jewish thinking. But as we know from the New Testament, not all Jews accepted this.

The Sadducees declined to accept the doctrine of resurrection because they had made a cosy and comfortable concordat with the ruling power and were prepared to let things go on as they were. The doctrine of resurrection was most decidedly a revolutionary and subversive doctrine because it implied that things, as they stood, were not the last word. We know that on this issue Jesus sided decisively with the Pharisees and against the Sadducees, and taught the resurrection of the body.

At the time of Jesus himself the holy land had for centuries past been desecrated by pagan armies, the Temple desecrated, the Law flouted, the rule of God denied and his people subjugated to the humiliation of slavery. It was a time of smouldering fomentation beneath the surface, always leading to the question: 'How long do we have to wait before God intervenes to fulfil his promises?'

We know from the Gospels that Jesus in his own person knew himself to be the presence of the rule and kingdom of God. The central message he brought to the world was that the rule of God was at hand. The hour had come. The crucial moment of judgment and redemption had arrived.

It is clear that to begin with Jesus sought to summon the

people of Israel as a whole to recognise the presence of this hour of judgment. They were urged to recognise the signs of the times and to fulfil the vocation for which God had called them: to be the suffering servant who manifested the glory of the kingdom of God. When Israel rejected this call, Jesus in a multitude of parables and teachings, warned that the absolute destruction of Israel was imminent. Here one thinks in particular of the parable of the tenants (Matthew 21:33–46). And with that destruction would come the crisis for the world. It is clear, however, that Jesus knew that in the end it was he himself, and he alone, who could and would fulfil the calling of Israel. That fulfilment would take place as he alone heeded God's call to be his servant, to suffer and to bear the sin of the world. He accordingly began to teach his disciples that he must suffer and die, but would rise again. And as we know, this is what actually happened.

But things did not turn out exactly as devout Jews thought they would. The resurrection of Jesus was not the end of history. The disciples at first thought it ought to be. They asked him, 'Lord, are you at this time going to restore the kingdom to Israel?' (Acts 1:6) They wanted to know if they were to have the kingdom then and there. If not, what was the meaning and point of all these things that had happened?

But Jesus told them they would have to wait. The day of final judgment was in the hands of the Father. But there would be a space, an interval of time between the resurrection of Jesus and the final end. There would be a time for the gospel to be disseminated throughout all nations, a time to repent and prepare for the day of judgment. How long that time would be the Father alone knew.

The disciples were taught to understand that they had been entrusted with the secret of the resurrection, that the death of Jesus was not the defeat of God's kingdom. On the contrary it was the victory. So this delay of the final judgment was to allow time for the gospel to be preached to all nations and to give them time to repent. As to the length of the delay, it was not for them to know. Jesus said, 'No-one knows about that day or hour, not even the angels in heaven, nor the Son, but only the Father' (Matthew 24:36).

What Jesus says of that momentous day is both that it is immediate and yet its timing is uncertain. There are parables and sayings of Jesus which suggest the end is imminent. Others stress the need for patience – there is no certain day.

Time and again, Jesus makes use of the image of the watchman. His job is to stay awake and alert throughout the night, and for hour after hour nothing might happen. But suddenly the decisive moment arrives when the master appears and all have to be ready immediately. So it is this combination of alertness and patience which corresponds to the fact that the final day is immediate, and yet at the same time we do not know when it will be.

Many modern New Testament scholars have looked only at those sayings of Jesus which speak of the immediacy and have then concluded that since two thousand years have passed, Jesus was simply mistaken. But this is the result of reading only half of the evidence. Indeed, it is extraordinary to me that contemporary New Testament scholars talk almost unanimously in this way. This is despite the fact that it is impossible to understand why the early church continued to spread the words and sayings of Jesus when they supposedly already knew or suspected that he was fundamentally mistaken.

What does the gospel teach us of the understanding of the end? I think it is summed up most beautifully in that verse at the beginning of the first letter of Peter: 'Praise be to the God and Father of our Lord Jesus Christ! In his great mercy he has given us new birth into a living hope through the resurrection of Jesus Christ from the dead, and into an inheritance that can never perish, spoil or fade – kept in heaven for you' (1 Peter 1:3–4). Those words are a wonderful summary of what has been accomplished.

There is a sense of hope which is not simply expressed as the desire for something in the future, which may or may not occur, but which we very much want to happen. It is not hope in that weak and vague sense which we so often use, but hope in the sense of absolute confidence: eagerly awaiting something that is assured, even though we do not know the day of its coming. In the words of the letter to the Hebrews, it is a hope that is 'an anchor for the soul' (Hebrews 6:19). It is unshakeable in its solidity. That is what we have been given. The resurrection of Jesus Christ is the pledge that death and sin have been conquered. We know that the end is the victory of God in Jesus Christ.

We must understand the future in a different way. Our

contemporary model of understanding the future has been around for the past two centuries or so. It attempts to paint a picture of a solid future, a future of hoped for continuing progress, rather than to suggest that we are peering into an essentially unknown future. But whatever the skills and technological wizardry of our computer-aided forecasters, all that we really know is that we do not know the future. It can always be a total surprise. What we look forward to in the Christian vocabulary is not 'future' but 'advent': that someone is coming to meet us. The horizon of our acting and thinking is thus not some unknown future, some utopia in perhaps the thirtieth or fortieth century. Its perspective is not my own personal survival, but the coming of Jesus. That is what we look forward to, that is the model, that is our horizon.

What do we envisage when we look to the future? What vista of an imagined future lies before us? Without doubt the answer is that momentous image of Jesus coming as the bearer of God's final victory and judgment. This means that our actions are not, so to speak, to be understood as creating or building the kingdom of God, as people used to say a few decades ago. It is not that our actions directly fulfil God's purpose for history as a whole. We know that our actions are ambivalent, confused and contradictory, and that even our good intentions often lead to results quite different from what was intended. No, the meaning of our actions should be understood essentially as 'acted prayers' for the kingdom. We pray, 'Your kingdom come.' But our actions are simply those prayers put into action, and they are offered to God to make of them what he will in his own providential design.

None of the geometrical patterns that I mentioned at the beginning is a satisfactory model. There is the cyclical pattern to which I have referred, and by contrast some theologians have suggested that the biblical pattern is linear. But if I may say so, this is not right. If it was truly a linear pattern then we would certainly have no part in the final victory of God's purpose. It really is not something that can be described in geometrical terms, but only personal terms. There is no direct road from the here and now to the kingdom of God. The path winds down into the valley, reaching into the depths of desolation that Jesus alone knew. Only from out of those depths – of the crucified, humiliated and defeated Jesus – does God raise up the new creation.

The resurrection of Jesus, from the degradation and defeat of the grave, is the pledge that out of the ruins of all that we bring about in history, God will raise a new creation. 'A new heaven and a new earth . . . for the old order of things has passed away' (Revelation 21:1, 4). There is no straight line. If you want a geometrical pattern, it goes right down. And only then, when God raises it up, does it reach its climax.

Basically, I am saying that geometrical patterns will not work. It is a personal relationship. Our actions are to be understood as acted prayers for the kingdom. We offer not just prayer but action. We offer ourselves to God. And because there is only one perfect sacrifice, that of Jesus on the cross, it follows that those actions which will be accepted, honoured and raised up by God, will be those we undertake for the sake, and as members of, the body of Christ – acted prayers through Jesus Christ our Lord. That is the model we must adopt in order to understand the relationship between our actions now and their connection to the end of all things.

There is that wonderful story of Jeremiah as he lay in prison (Jeremiah 32). One of his relatives came and told him that a piece of family property was up for sale and he ought to buy it. This land was under enemy occupation and the Babylonian armies were about to take and destroy Jerusalem and carry its people into captivity. Nevertheless, Jeremiah paid seventeen shekels of silver for it and then he asked himself the question we have all asked at times in our life, 'Why did I do such a stupid thing?' God answered him that in the end the land would be redeemed. Jeremiah took a risk which in relation to his current situation was seemingly absurd. But it was the action that corresponded to what God had promised. In fact it was the model for all our action, then and now.

Even in situations which seem hopeless, when acts of love, forgiveness or kindness seem irrelevant, we still undertake those actions. This is not because we think these acts are going to be immediately effective in some way, but because they correspond to what God has promised. They are therefore realistic actions corresponding to the ultimate reality, and are accordingly acted prayers for the kingdom of God.

I return to my question: What is it we see when we look forward? It is not merely an indefinite and unknowable future,

but an advent. He shall come again in glory to judge the
living and the dead. He will come again and he will come as
Judge. If there is no final judgment, then the words 'right'
and 'wrong' have no meaning. If in the end 'right' and 'wrong'
add up to the same thing then they are meaningless words.
Morality is reduced to my personal chosen values. But we
cannot eliminate this word 'judgment' from our thinking:
' . . . he is the one whom God appointed as judge of the living
and the dead' (Acts 10:42). The reason for that is that he is
'the light of the world'. St John's Gospel says, 'This is the
verdict [judgment]: Light has come into the world, but people
loved darkness instead of light because their deeds were evil'
(John 3:19).

The essential point about light is that in its glare things
are seen as they really are, and in the end everything will be
seen as it really is. There will in the end be no confusion
between right and wrong, between truth and lies. If we side-
step that central element of our faith then the words 'right'
and 'wrong' become meaningless. When we assert that a thing
is wrong, even if everybody denies it, what we are saying is
that in the end, in the light of Jesus, it will be seen that it
is wrong. Otherwise, the word is devoid of meaning.

When we speak about judgment, we must remember that
in all of the parables of Jesus about the last judgment, the
emphasis is on surprise. Those who thought that they were
in suddenly find themselves out. And those who thought they
were always doomed to be outside, find themselves in. 'So
the last will be first, and the first will be last' (Matthew

20:16). All things are finally in God's hands and we are warned that judgment, and the time for it, belongs to God alone.

Our creed goes on, 'I believe in . . . the communion of saints, the forgiveness of sins, the resurrection of the body, and the life everlasting.' The New Testament says little about what must always be a tantalising mystery of what happens to the believers who die in the faith before the end has come. Where are they and what happens to them? The New Testament is very reticent about it. In the New Testament all the emphasis is on that final victory, the resurrection of the dead, the judgment, the kingdom and the glory and the new heavens and the new earth. But there are hints, especially in that wonderful passage in Hebrews 11 and 12 where they are spoken of as 'a cloud of witnesses' (Hebrews 12:1) that surround us, looking to Jesus, with us looking to Jesus and waiting for the day of his glory.

In our Protestant reaction against an excessive concern about those who have died in faith in the Roman Catholic Church, many of us have been insufficiently explicit about this. I think that the communion of the saints, those who have gone before us, are still surrounding us as 'a cloud of witnesses' looking to Jesus. I think this despite the fact that we know little of their state and the Scriptures do not say much about them. And we can rejoice in their communion. Remember them, thank God for them, as a regular and important part of our prayers. This has certainly become an increasingly important part of my own prayers.

The Scriptures teach us that the resurrection of the body is the end and not the pagan idea of the immortality of the soul. The scriptural idea of the resurrection of the body is part of the whole vision of new heavens and a new earth, a fresh creation in which all that God had purposed for the creation of the world and his human family is redeemed and consummated in his kingdom.

Finally, the life everlasting. This is the communion in the life of the blessed Trinity for which Jesus prays on the night of his passion, 'That they may be one, as we are one: I in them and you in me. May they be brought to complete unity' (John 17:23). This is the prayer that we are permitted to enter into and in which we may live forever in the glory, the joy and love of the triune God. This is something that passes our understanding and yet continually beckons us as the true goal of our being.

Time and again, the New Testament reminds us that in this interval of time between the resurrection and the second coming, there is given to us a foretaste of that joy: the presence of the Holy Spirit. This is the pledge, the first fruit, the *arrabon* – to use that ancient word of the kingdom – not the whole reality, but a real taste of that bliss and freedom, and of the glory that belongs to God. These things are given to us so that we may possess in the external world of history the fact of the resurrection, and in the life of our own souls the presence of the Spirit as the double pledge that in the end, God reigns. And to him be the praise.

More on Lesslie Newbigin

If you have enjoyed this book, you may like to know more about Lesslie Newbigin and his work. You will find two internet sites of particular help:

www.newbigin.net carries a searchable database containing a comprehensive list of this prolific author's writings and of substantial engagements with him. The site also contains the text (also searchable) of over fifty articles written by him.

www.gospel-culture.org.uk is the website of 'The Gospel and Our Culture Network' in Great Britain. This organisation was started by Lesslie Newbigin and its website contains a whole section on him, together with a complete archive of past newsletters including articles by him. The website also offers links to sister organisations in North America and New Zealand.

The Alpha Course

The Alpha Course is an opportunity to explore the meaning of life. It is a ten-week course which started at Holy Trinity Brompton in 1976 and is now run by thousands of churches in many countries across the world.

Alpha International have produced many publications to help churches run the course, including:

Alpha Introductory Video   ISBN 1 8988 3850 X £4.99
An introduction designed for church leaders.

Questions of Life   ISBN 0 8547 6738 X £5.99
The talks of the Alpha course in book form.

How to Run the Alpha Course ISBN 1 9040 7416 2 £14.99
Video
This video provides the essential foundation or guidelines for anyone thinking of setting up an Alpha Course. It includes the conference talks on the principles and practicalities of the course.

The Alpha Course Video Set   ISBN 1 9027 5089 6 £89.95
The fifteen talks on video.

The Alpha Course Manual   ISBN 1 9040 7423 5 £1.50

Why Jesus?   ISBN 1 8988 3845 3 £0.40
An evangelistic booklet for those who are starting to think about the Christian faith.

Other publications and courses

Searching Issues (available as a course with book, audio and manual)
                                        Book ISBN 0 8547 6739 8 £5.99
Nicky Gumbel tackles the seven most common objections to the Christian faith. Includes suffering, other religions and sex before marriage. (Individual chapters are also available.)

A Life Worth Living (available as a course with book, video, audio, manual and leaders' manual)
                                        Book ISBN 0 8547 6740 1 £5.99
Based on the book of Philippians, *A Life Worth Living* is aimed at those starting out in the Christian life, showing how it is possible to live the Christian life positively, joyfully and practically.

The Marriage Course
The Marriage Course is a series of eight sessions and is designed to help married couples strengthen their relationship. The course is appropriate for any married couple, whether or not they are churchgoers.

The Marriage Course   ISBN 1 9040 7410 3 £4.99
Introductory Video
This video gives an insight into The Marriage Course for those who may be thinking of starting a course.

The Marriage Book   ISBN 1 9027 5026 8 £5.99
Full of practical advice, it is easy to read and designed to prepare, build and even mend marriages.

The Marriage Book and The Marriage Course were written by Nicky and Sila Lee. They have been married for over twenty years and are on the staff at Holy Trinity Brompton.

Further information/
Mail Order Brochure

To order the above, or to request a free mail order brochure with full details of all our publications, please call the Alpha Publications Hotline:

0845 7581 278 (all calls at local rate)

To order from overseas:
Tel +44 1228 512 512
Fax +44 1228 514 949

Or contact your National Alpha Office.

If you would like further information on any of our products, please contact:
Publications Department
Alpha International
Holy Trinity Brompton
Brompton Road, London SW7 1JA
Tel: 0845 644 7544 Fax: 020 7584 8536
E-mail: publications@htb.org.uk
Website: alphacourse.org